T0316548

Cambridge Elements ≡

Elements in Ethics
edited by
Ben Eggleston
University of Kansas
Dale E. Miller
Old Dominion University, Virginia

PARFIT'S ETHICS

Richard Yetter Chappell
University of Miami

CAMBRIDGE
UNIVERSITY PRESS

CAMBRIDGE
UNIVERSITY PRESS

University Printing House, Cambridge CB2 8BS, United Kingdom

One Liberty Plaza, 20th Floor, New York, NY 10006, USA

477 Williamstown Road, Port Melbourne, VIC 3207, Australia

314–321, 3rd Floor, Plot 3, Splendor Forum, Jasola District Centre,
New Delhi – 110025, India

79 Anson Road, #06–04/06, Singapore 079906

Cambridge University Press is part of the University of Cambridge.

It furthers the University's mission by disseminating knowledge in the pursuit of
education, learning, and research at the highest international levels of excellence.

www.cambridge.org
Information on this title: www.cambridge.org/9781108730532
DOI: 10.1017/9781108582377

© Richard Yetter Chappell 2021

First published 2021

A catalogue record for this publication is available from the British Library.

ISBN 978-1-108-73053-2 Paperback
ISSN 2516-4031 (online)
ISSN 2516-4023 (print)

Parfit's Ethics

Elements in Ethics

DOI: 10.1017/9781108582377
First published online: April 2021

Richard Yetter Chappell
University of Miami

Author for correspondence: Richard Yetter Chappell, r.chappell@gmail.com

Abstract: Derek Parfit (1942–2017) was one of the most important and influential moral philosophers of the late twentieth and early twenty-first centuries. This Element offers a critical introduction to his wide-ranging ethical thought, focussing especially on his two most significant works, *Reasons and Persons* (1984) and *On What Matters* (2011), and their contribution to the consequentialist moral tradition. Topics covered include: rationality and objectivity, distributive justice, self-defeating moral theories, Parfit's Triple Theory (according to which consequentialism, contractualism, and Kantian ethics ultimately converge), personal identity, and population ethics.

Keywords: Parfit, consequentialism, ethical theory, population ethics, distributive justice

ISBNs: 9781108730532 (PB), 9781108582377 (OC)
ISSNs: 2516-4031 (online), 2516-4023 (print)

Contents

1 Introduction

Derek Parfit (1942–2017) was one of the most important and influential moral philosophers of the late twentieth and early twenty-first centuries. This Element seeks to introduce the reader to his wide-ranging ethical thought, focussing especially on his two most significant works: *Reasons and Persons* (1984) and *On What Matters* (2011a).

Parfit was centrally concerned about objectivity in ethics and practical rationality. Section 2 of this Element discusses his arguments against common-place "subjectivist" assumptions, and briefly touches on his meta-ethical views regarding the nature of objective morality.

The next three sections address Parfit's contributions to the consequentialist tradition within ethical theory. Consequentialists generally regard actions as morally significant insofar as they produce good or bad outcomes. *Act Consequentialism* directs us to maximize the good. *Utilitarianism* is a form of consequentialism which further specifies that the good consists in the well-being of sentient beings. *Act Utilitarianism* thus directs us to maximize aggregate well-being. This simple view has faced many pressing objections. Parfit's ethical theory can be understood in part as a reaction to these objections.

For example, egalitarians have objected that utilitarianism neglects the *distribution* of well-being across the population. Some object to allowing a single great harm to one to be outweighed by many small benefits to others. Section 3 relates Parfit's innovative response to such objections: to argue that the underlying intuitions are best accommodated by a modest revision to utilitarianism so as to give extra weight or priority to the well-being of the worse off. It also explores whether we can further improve upon Parfit's revisions here.

Others have raised concerns about the potentially self-effacing nature of consequentialist views. If believing some other view would have better consequences, does that suggest that consequentialism is self-defeating in any problematic sense? Is it always best to act according to the best rules? Section 4 discusses how Parfit's early work shed important light on such structural questions. Perhaps one of the most interesting results to emerge from Parfit's work here is an argument to the effect that it is common-sense morality, rather than impartial consequentialism, that faces the greatest risk of being (problematically) self-defeating.

A prominent objection to Act Consequentialism is that it too easily permits intuitively heinous acts such as the killing of innocent people (if so acting would save a larger number from similar harms). *Rule Consequentialism* directs us to follow, instead, the rules whose general acceptance would have the best consequences. This seems likely to include a rule against killing the innocent. Section

5 critically examines the prospects for Rule Consequentialism, alongside Parfit's ambitious arguments for the "Triple Theory", according to which the best forms of Kantianism, Contractualism, and Rule Consequentialism ultimately converge.

Our final two sections look at some of Parfit's most distinctive work. Section 6 explores questions of personal identity through time, and Parfit's arguments for the striking claim that identity is not what matters in survival. Section 7 offers a brief overview of key issues in population ethics – a new subfield of ethics that is largely built upon Parfit's seminal insights. In both cases, we find that incredible-seeming claims can be supported by arguments that seem almost inescapable. I find few philosophical puzzles to be as gripping – yet slippery! – and rewarding to grapple with as those contained within these pages.

Note: I have written this Element as an *opinionated guide* to Parfit's ethics, rather than attempting a neutral exegesis. Throughout, I try to explain what I find most valuable in his work, as well as what I think he may have been wrong about (and why). But the reader is encouraged to question my verdicts – and Parfit's too. We make progress in philosophy by questioning and probing each other's arguments and ideas. While I believe that this Element contains some important truths, my strongest hope is that it provokes readers to engage philosophically with Parfit's arguments and ideas, no matter whether they ultimately agree with them.

2 Rationality and Objectivity

Parfit was centrally concerned with questions about practical rationality and what we ought, all things considered, to do.[1] As Parfit uses these terms, they might come apart in cases of ignorance or misinformation. An agent might rationally act on mistaken beliefs, and thereby fail to do what they *ought* (given the facts) to do. But, in what follows, I will focus on cases in which the agent knows all the relevant facts, so that we can speak interchangeably of what they "ought" to do or what it would be "rational" for them to do.

It's common in our broader culture to implicitly equate practical rationality with self-interest. According to *Rational Egoism*, or the "Self-Interest Theory", what each person ultimately has most reason to do is whatever would make their own life go best, on the whole. A central concern of Parfit (1984), in the second of the book's four parts, is to undermine this common view. Parfit compellingly argues that rational egoism cannot sustain itself against simultaneous attacks

---

[1] *Practical* rationality concerns the rationality of choice and action – aspects of our agency that seek to *change* the world – in contrast to *theoretical* rationality which concerns the rationality of judgement and belief – aspects of agency that seek to *accurately represent* the world.

from two sides, and must ultimately give way to a competing view that is either more objective or else more subjective.

Subjectivist views hold that normative reasons are grounded in the agent's desires (which are not themselves rationally evaluable, at least on the most straightforward versions of the view). Practical rationality is thus limited to *instrumental rationality*, or the evaluation of means in terms of their effectiveness at achieving whatever the agent's chosen ends might be. This view is importantly distinct from Rational Egoism, as agents might care about more than just their own interests, and – most strikingly – they might fail to care about their own interests. While we will see that Parfit rejects Rational Egoism as unduly restrictive, subjectivism risks being too lax an account of practical rationality, as grossly imprudent behaviour tends to strike us as irrational. That is, a modicum of concern for your future interests strikes us as required by rationality, suggesting that – contra subjectivism – at least some of our ultimate ends are rationally evaluable after all.

Parfit is thus led to the view that some things objectively matter, in the sense that we all have normative reason to care about them, no matter what desires we happen to have to begin with. On this view, when we fail to care appropriately about the things that really matter, we are making a genuine *mistake*, and are rationally criticizable in much the same way that someone who fails to apportion their beliefs to the evidence is rationally criticizable.

While the central concern of this section is to explain the arguments outlined above, we will close by briefly exploring the metaphysics and epistemology of normativity that Parfit believed necessary to support objectivity in normative ethics.

2.1 Rational Egoism

In requiring agents to always prioritize their self-interest over any competing concerns, Rational Egoism is a strikingly restrictive theory. As Parfit (1984, chapter 6) observes, it surely seems like we can reasonably care about things other than just our own interests. We may, for example, care about other people, or about achieving some magnificent goal, more than we care about our own future happiness or overall interests.[2] Parfit thus proposes the following simple counterexample to Rational Egoism:

---

[2] Even if one thinks that these things would then count as being among one's interests, the point remains that we could reasonably care about them to a degree that is disproportionate in comparison to the amount that they contribute to our well-being. We may thus reasonably prefer an outcome in which we are overall worse off, but this special goal is better achieved, over an alternative in which we are personally better off but fail in this goal.

> *My Heroic Death.* I choose to die in a way that I know will be painful, but will save the lives of several other people. I am doing what, knowing the facts and thinking clearly, I most want to do. . . . I also know that I am doing what will be worse for me. If I did not sacrifice my life, to save these other people, I would not be haunted by remorse. The rest of my life would be well worth living. (Parfit 1984, 132)

Rational Egoism must condemn the agent's choice in *My Heroic Death* as irrational, as they knowingly go against what is in their self-interest. But given that the agent is fully informed, thinking clearly, and acting in a way that is morally admirable, it is difficult to see any fair, non-dogmatic basis for insisting that their choice is irrational, just because they chose to prioritize others' interests over their own. Unless supported by some incredibly compelling theoretical rationale, the implausibility of Rational Egoism's verdicts in cases like this gives us good grounds to reject the view in favour of some more permissive alternative.

Parfit (1984) goes on, in chapter 7, to undermine Rational Egoism at a more theoretical level. Compare the following three principles:

(A) No individual preference is intrinsically irrational (just in virtue of its content), not even preferring a lesser benefit over a much greater one.

(B) It's irrational to prefer a lesser benefit over a much greater benefit, merely on the grounds that the former occurs *now* whereas the latter occurs *later*.

(C) It's irrational to prefer a lesser benefit over a much greater benefit, merely on the grounds that the former accrues to *you* whereas the latter accrues to *another*.

Rational Egoists accept principle (B) but reject both (A) and (C). Parfit argues that this is an unstable position, as there are good theoretical grounds for treating (B) and (C) alike. Parfit's basic idea is that there is a kind of formal *analogy* between "I" and "now", or between *agent* relativity and *temporal* relativity. When Rational Egoism dictates that we must be *temporally neutral* (giving equal weight to our interests at all times) but *agent relative* (giving more weight to ourselves than to others), it reveals itself to be what Parfit calls an "incompletely relative" theory. A theory is on sounder structural ground, Parfit believes, when it is either fully relative or fully neutral, treating both these dimensions of variation alike.

Why does Parfit think this? One way to understand his core insight is to notice that choices are made not only by particular agents but also at particular times. (It may be helpful to think of the deliberating agent as a "momentary self", distinct from the various "future selves" that will replace them at later times.) Just as a deliberator may ask, 'Why should *I* sacrifice my interests just so that some *others* may benefit?', so we may imagine them asking, 'Why should *I now* sacrifice my *current* interests just so that my *future* selves may benefit?'. If the former question is thought to raise a serious challenge to altruistic requirements, parity of reasoning would suggest that the latter question should be considered similarly challenging to requirements of prudence.

Rational Egoists might seek to defend requirements of prudence by appealing to the objective features of normatively significant phenomena such as pain. Pain matters because of how it feels, and the felt badness of pain is not affected by mere differences in timing. This is, Parfit suggests, an excellent defence of (B). But it is not one that the Rational Egoist can comfortably appeal to, for analogous reasoning would equally support principle (C). After all, the felt badness of pain is likewise unaffected by mere differences in *who* feels it.

Rational Egoism is thus undermined on both intuitive and theoretical grounds. We should instead accept a theory of practical rationality that is either more subjective or more impartial. Parfit's arguments here provide a nice demonstration of the power of philosophy to force a rethinking of prevalent assumptions. As a result of such arguments, philosophers now overwhelmingly reject this view. The same cannot be said of Parfit's next target, however, which enjoys much greater philosophical influence.

2.2 Normative Subjectivism

Normative subjectivists claim that we have reason to do whatever will fulfil our ultimate (non-instrumental) desires. On the purest version of this view, agents may be susceptible to rational criticism when they fail to effectively pursue their goals, but the goals themselves are immune from rational criticism. As Hume (1739, 2.3.3.6) famously declared, ' 'Tis not contrary to reason to prefer the destruction of the whole world to the scratching of my finger.'

Parfit disagrees, as it seems to make perfect sense to criticize desires, and not just beliefs, as "crazy" or irrational. To illustrate, Parfit (1984, 124) imagines an agent with *Future-Tuesday Indifference*, who 'would choose a painful operation on the following Tuesday rather than a much less painful operation on the following Wednesday'. The imagined agent knows he will subsequently regret it, but simply doesn't care – about either his future agony or the associated regret. Such an agent seems less than perfectly rational. Many of us would probably describe such a pattern of concern as "senseless" or even "crazy". As Parfit sums up his case: 'Preferring the *worse* of two pains, for *no* reason, is irrational.'

Future-Tuesday Indifference shows us that there's more to practical rationality than just taking the effective means to whatever your ends may be. Our ends themselves are open to rational evaluation. At a minimum, there's some rational pressure to treat like cases alike, or avoid arbitrary distinctions (Smith 1994): if pain is worth avoiding on other days, and it feels no different on those calendar days arbitrarily designated to be "Tuesdays", then we rationally ought to regard Tuesday pain as similarly worth avoiding.

This is to suggest a *structural* rational requirement – a requirement governing combinations of desires. Such structural requirements by themselves do not yet establish that any desire is *intrinsically* irrational; they just specify that certain combinations of desires cannot rationally be held together. Sophisticated subjectivists might happily insist, in this way, that whatever desires you have must cohere together and avoid arbitrary distinctions, while retaining their core commitment to the idea that any desire *could* be rationally held (in isolation, or with the right companion desires).

Parfit's objection to subjectivism can be pressed further: avoiding arbitrary distinctions by becoming indifferent to *all* future agony would simply compound the error of the Future-Tuesday-Indifferent agent. To restore rationality, it isn't enough to be consistent. If sufficiently wrong-headed, that might just make you more consistently irrational. To do better, we must respond to evaluatively significant features of the world in the ways that they actually merit.

Parfit (2011a, 76) thus affirms as a *categorical* requirement of reason that 'We all have a reason to want to avoid, and to try to avoid, all future agony.' You may wonder: What about masochists for whom some degree of pain can serve, instrumentally, to bring them pleasure? They can simply weigh their reason to seek pleasure against the reason to avoid pain, and see which is the greater. Parfit need not deny that there are possible cases in which the reasons to avoid pain are outweighed by sufficient instrumental benefits. But to simplify the discussion, it will help to focus on cases in which there are no such instrumental benefits in play. So let's interpret "agony" here as meaning a state that is experienced as *entirely* negative in valence. So understood, Parfit's datum – that all agents have reason to want to avoid future agony – seems difficult to deny.

Normative subjectivists have trouble accommodating Parfit's datum, however. For their view seems to imply that agents never really have *reason to want* anything: our wants are simply taken as given, and the subjectivist instead focusses on what we have reason to *do*, namely, effectively pursue whatever it is that we antecedently want.[3]

---

[3] This raises a puzzle: Why would we have reason to pursue some end that we have no reason to want? *Hypothetical imperatives* of the form, "If you want X, you should do Y", present relations of normative inherence: *given* that X is worth pursuing, then Y is too. But a view on which there

Returning to Parfit's counterexample: if someone presently happens not to care about future agony, then (subjectivism implies) they've no present reason to try to avoid such future agony. That seems wrong. So we have two grounds here for rejecting subjectivism: it falsely implies (i) that agents have no reason to *want* to avoid future agony, and (ii) that some possible agents have no reason to *act* so as to avoid future agony. This is Parfit's *Agony Argument*.

Sobel (2011, 63) responds that subjectivists might yet accept a *Reasons Transfer Principle* according to which: 'If one will later have a reason to get O, then one now has a reason to facilitate the later getting of O.' If so, the agent's future reason to avoid concurrent agony provides the present agent with a reason to avoid that future agony. It's an interesting question whether we should consider the Reasons Transfer Principle to be compatible with the spirit of subjectivism. (It requires positing a kind of normative authority that goes beyond the agent's present deliberative perspective, thus conflicting with the traditional "internalist" strain of subjectivism associated with Williams (1981).) But even if (some) subjectivists can in this way avoid the problematic verdict about our reasons for action, they still face the first part of the objection: that their view appears to be incompatible with our having *reasons to want* to avoid future agony in the first place.

Perhaps it's psychologically inevitable that future agony will entail some thwarted future desires (assuming that agony necessarily either involves or generates a concurrent desire for the agonizing experience to cease). By subjectivist lights, those future desires may generate future reasons to avoid being in agony, and by the Reasons Transfer Principle, those future reasons may likewise give the present agent reason to avoid the future agony (if they can). But what is the status of the future desires that started all this? For subjectivists, they generate reasons just in virtue of being desires that the agent has – their specific content is irrelevant to their reason-giving force. So the agent may have equally strong desires to experience agony (without enjoying it in any way), or to robotically count blades of grass, any of which would end up having the same normative significance as the desire to avoid agony. This seems a troubling verdict: many of us, at least, would be inclined to think that the desire to avoid agony is *warranted* in a way that a gratuitous desire to experience agony, by contrast, is not. Such considerations may help to push us towards a more objective normative view.

Subjectivists like to point out that we often have reason to do what we desire. If desires ground reasons, that would certainly explain the correlation. But it is

---

are *only* hypothetical imperatives is effectively a form of normative nihilism – no more productive than an irrigation system without any liquid to flow through it. Or so it seems to me.

not the only available explanation. Parfit instead explains away the correlation: first, our desires might indirectly affect our reasons, for example, by making it the case that we would *enjoy* some activity (or else be unhappy without it). On any plausible objective view, happiness is one of the things that objectively matters, so it is to be expected that we will typically have reason to fulfil our desires if this would make us happier. Second, our desires may often *track* the things that really matter, or are objectively good (in much the same way that our beliefs track the truth). Candidate objective goods include things such as happiness, achievement, success in one's central life goals, friendship and loving relationships, and helping others in need. It should come as no surprise that reasonable people tend to desire and pursue such ends, if (as many objectivists believe) they are genuinely good things that *merit* our attraction and pursuit.

To properly test our intuitions about subjectivism, then, we must consider special cases in which desire-satisfaction diverges from happiness and other candidate objective goods. In such cases, it no longer seems so plausible that desire-satisfaction is the only thing that matters. A major remaining challenge for the Parfitian objectivist, however, is to assuage our theoretical misgivings about how anything *could* really matter.

2.3 Objective Normativity

Objections to normative realism (the idea that some things really matter) come in two broad flavours: metaphysical and epistemic. The former concern the nature of *mattering*, or how normative properties could really *exist*. Next, assuming that objective normative truths are somehow "out there", epistemic objections remain about how we could possibly come to *know* them.

Mackie (1977, 38) famously objected that 'If there were objective values, then they would be entities ... of a very strange sort, utterly different from anything else in the universe.'[4] Parfit (2011b, chapter 31) seeks to defang such metaphysical qualms by denying that objective values (or normative properties more generally) would have to exist 'in the universe' at all. Nor do they exist in some separate, ghostly Platonic realm. That is still to treat them too much on the model of concrete objects that exist in space and time. Instead, Parfit suggests, abstract entities like numbers and objective values exist in a 'non-ontological' sense. True claims about numbers and values are as true as true can be, but – Parfit insists – these truths 'have no positive

---

[4] As Kirchin (2010) argues, it's not so clear just what Mackie's target is. I focus here on objective values, broadly speaking, and ignore Mackie's misguided assumption that these would necessarily have a magnetic pull on our motivation.

ontological implications' (Parfit (2011b, 479). This is Parfit's *Non-Metaphysical Cognitivism* in a nutshell.[5]

Parfit thus hopes to secure the best of both worlds: the objectivity of robust normative realism, without the ontological costs. Whether this is a coherent position is, unfortunately, less clear.[6] Parfit (2011b, 479) claims that abstract entities 'are not a kind of entity about which it is a clear enough question whether, in some ontological sense, they exist, or are real, though they are not in space and time'. He seems to draw from this the conclusion that we can comfortably rely upon abstract objects at no theoretical cost. I wonder if a better conclusion would be that the theoretical costs of positing abstract objects are, as yet, *unclear*. But even this more moderate conclusion may be consoling in its own way. For it undermines the suggestion that there is anything *obviously* objectionable (or theoretically costly) about positing objective values.

Some sceptics have thought that objective values would be more problematic than other abstract objects. Mackie (1977, 40) supposed that they must be imbued with a kind of magical motivating force, claiming that '[a]n objective good would be sought by anyone who was acquainted with it'. Parfit (2011b, 268), by contrast, takes great care to distinguish motivating and normative reasons. We are substantively irrational when we fail to be moved by (known) normative reasons. But there is no force in the universe that prevents us from being irrational. Normativity is causally inert, on Parfit's view: it marks what truly ought to be done, but it cannot push us to do it. Their causal inefficacy makes Parfit's non-natural properties more metaphysically innocent (being compatible with the principle that physical effects can only stem from physical causes), but perhaps more epistemically puzzling.

If abstract objects cannot causally influence physical objects such as our brains, how can we possibly know anything about them? Parfit (2011b, chapter 32) suggests that causally responsive perceptual faculties are only required for detecting *contingent* truths, which could have been otherwise. Following Sidgwick (1907), Parfit suggests that the necessary truths of logic, mathematics, and philosophy are *self-evident* in the sense that full rational understanding of the claim in question gives one sufficient justification for believing it: no causal interaction or external evidence is required.[7]

---

[5] Parfit (2016) seeks to develop this meta-ethical view, together with Railton's naturalism and Gibbard's expressivism, so that all three converge. We haven't space to explore this here, but interested readers may look to reviews of the volume such as (Roojen 2017).

[6] Cf. Suikkanen (2017) and Mintz-Woo (2018). Related views are defended in Scanlon (2014) and Skorupski (2010).

[7] Indeed, the a priori nature of fundamental moral truths can be used to argue against metaethical naturalism, as per Howard and Laskowski (2019) and (Chappell n.d.a).

To appreciate that 2+2=4, or that pain is bad, you don't need to run a scientific experiment to better reveal the causal structure of the world. Once you've acquired the relevant concepts, you just need to think clearly. Not all self-evident truths are so obvious as these examples, and we are all fallible, imperfectly rational beings. So people may disagree about what is truly self-evident, and sometimes get it wrong. But the core suggestion is nonetheless that careful thinking *may* see us right, and at any rate is the only hope we have, so we might as well give it our best shot.[8]

3 Distributive Justice

Traditional consequentialist views (such as utilitarianism) are commonly criticized for neglecting *distributional* concerns. The most straightforward of these concerns involves the value of equality: Would it not seem better to have everyone content than to have half the population ecstatic while the other half is miserable, even if global net happiness is the same either way? Others object to aggregating different people's interests together, so that small benefits to sufficiently many might together outweigh great harms to a few. Finally, some have raised concerns about whether consequentialism can adequately account for obligations not to contribute to collective harms (such as pollution or climate change). In this section, we will examine Parfit's contributions to addressing these challenges.

3.1 Equality and Priority

Many people are drawn to the *egalitarian* idea that it is in itself bad if some people are worse off than others.[9] Parfit (1997) invites us to imagine a *Divided World*, where each half of the population lives in complete isolation from, and ignorance of, the other half. This stipulation allows us to bracket any merely *instrumental* effects of inequality, and focus instead on whether inequality is bad *in itself*, even apart from any bad effects it might typically have. Now compare the following two states of affairs:

(1) half at 100 units of well-being; half at 200
(2) everyone at 145.

Many people are drawn to the view that (2) is better than (1), even though it contains less well-being in total. If we take this evaluative claim to be a moral

---

[8] I further defend a version of Parfit's moral epistemology against sceptical worries in (Chappell 2017a).

[9] For simplicity, I focus here on the view that Parfit calls 'Telic Egalitarianism'. There is an alternative view, 'Deontic Egalitarianism', which directs us to remedy unjust inequalities, but does not count inequality as making outcomes *worse*. See Parfit (1997, 207–10) for more detail.

datum, we may wonder how best to explain it. One candidate answer is offered by egalitarianism: (1) is made worse by the presence of inequality, and this is sufficient to outweigh the slight gain in utility (total well-being) that it boasts over state of affairs (2). Parfit offers a different answer, but before we get to that, let's consider his main objection to egalitarianism.

Parfit notes that egalitarianism is susceptible to the *levelling down objection*. After all, there are in principle two ways to remedy an inequality: improve the lot of the worse off, or make things worse for the better off. There are obvious reasons to prefer the former, as that helps people, increasing utility as well as equality. But if inequality is bad in itself, then it follows that there is *something good* about reducing inequality as such, even if this is achieved via the latter route of "levelling down" or simply harming the better-off group without helping anyone. This dubious implication gives us reason to reject egalitarianism.

Rather than holding inequality to be bad in itself, Parfit suggests, we might instead get the desired result that (2) is better than (1) because we give *more weight* to the interests of the worse off. Perhaps increasing your well-being from 100 to 145 is simply *worth more* than increasing your well-being from 145 to 200. According to Parfit's *prioritarian* view, 'Benefiting people matters more the worse off these people are' (Parfit 1997, 213).

Crucially, prioritarianism is *non-comparative*. It holds that the moral importance of benefitting a person depends just on that person's absolute level of well-being. It does not matter how that person's level of well-being compares to that of others. (More priority weighting will be given to the interests of someone who is *even worse* off. But each person's respective priority weightings are explained by their respective absolute levels of well-being, rather than by the comparative fact that one was higher than the other.)

There is something theoretically attractive about this non-comparative perspective. It accounts for the special importance of improving the well-being of the badly off. And it does so without implying that it is in *any* way good in itself to reduce the well-being of the better off.

Parfit's prioritarianism may thus seem like a straightforward improvement over egalitarianism. But it does face challenges of its own. To bring this out, consider how a utilitarian might try to explain away our egalitarian intuitions. Utilitarians will often support more equal distributions of *resources* for instrumental reasons. After all, resources such as money tend to have *diminishing marginal utility*: the more you have, the less of a difference one more unit tends to make. A dollar is worth a lot more to a homeless person than to a millionaire, after all.

The funny thing about prioritarianism is that it seems to treat utility (well-being) itself as having diminishing marginal value. To illustrate, suppose for simplicity that prioritarianism applies to momentary rather than lifetime well-being. Now imagine that Joe has the option to provide himself with either a small benefit at a time when he is poorly off, or a greater benefit at a time when he is better off. By definition, the latter option benefits him more. But the (momentary) priority view implies that the former may be "more important". That is, *considering only this person's welfare, it might be better to do what is worse for him.* Could that really be right?

To extend the argument to target the lifetime version of prioritarianism, we must tweak the case to involve counterfactual rather than temporal comparisons. Suppose that Shmoe will be happier if a flipped coin lands heads, and can further grant himself either of two conditional benefits: a greater benefit in the event that the coin lands heads, or a small benefit in the event of tails. If benefits matter more to the worse off, and he's worse off in the event of tails, then the 50 per cent chance of a smaller benefit (conditional on tails) may be recommended by prioritarianism as better than the 50 per cent chance of a greater benefit. But that would not be the prudent choice.

To avoid such problems, utilitarians may agree with Parfit that our intuitions support prioritarianism, but then seek to give a debunking explanation of these intuitions rather than accepting them at face value. Experimental evidence suggests that our intuitive appreciation of the diminishing marginal utility of resources overgeneralizes when presented with a new kind of unit – a "unit of wellbeing" – with which we lack intuitive familiarity (Greene and Baron 2001).

Alternatively, some people might be drawn to the view that various basic goods (such as happiness), which directly contribute to well-being, have diminishing marginal utility, and then confuse this with the prioritarian claim. To ensure theoretical clarity, we must take care to distinguish the prioritarian idea that the interests of the worse off simply *matter* more, from the (utilitarian-compatible) idea that certain goods would constitute *a greater benefit* for the worse off, that is, make a greater difference to their (inherently equally important) interests. This latter view would have much the same practical implications as prioritarianism, but without the theoretical costs.

Either way, we are now in a position to accommodate many egalitarian intuitions without having to attribute intrinsic significance to relational equality per se.

3.2 Aggregation

Another standard challenge to traditional consequentialist views concerns its *aggregative* treatment of disparate interests. If one option would give tiny benefits to a great many people, whereas a second option would immensely help a single individual, consequentialists will standardly want to "add up" all the tiny benefits resulting from the first option to see whether, in aggregate, they outweigh the single great benefit. Some critics feel that this is the wrong way to approach trade-offs between different numbers of people. Some even go so far as to say that the numbers should not "count", or matter, at all.

Parfit's central contributions to this debate are found in his (2003) paper, 'Justifiability to Each Person', where he especially engages with Scanlon (1998). Scanlon motivates his anti-aggregative approach with the now famous *Transmitter Room* case, which Parfit summarizes as follows: 'Jones has suffered an accident in the transmitter room of a television station. To save Jones from an hour of severe pain, we would have to cancel part of the broadcast of a football game, which is giving pleasure to very many people' (Parfit 2003, 375).

Intuitively, it doesn't matter how many people are watching the football game; it's just *more important* to save Jones from suffering severe pain during this time. Why? One answer would be that we can't aggregate distinct interests, so all that's left to do is to satisfy whichever individual moral claim is strongest, namely, Jones's. But Parfit suggests an alternative explanation: perhaps we should help Jones because he is much worse off, and thus has greater moral priority. If the watchers were even worse off than Jones, then Parfit's explanation would fail, but he could instead insist that slightly improving the lot of billions of worse-off individuals really should be prioritized over offering great relief to a single individual who is already comparatively better off.

In line with this suggestion, Parfit argues that his prioritarian account is preferable to Scanlon's anti-aggregative approach in cases where the two diverge. We can see this by imagining cases in which the many smaller benefits would go to some of the worst-off individuals. By refusing to countenance aggregation, we would end up prioritizing a single large benefit to someone already well off, rather than (individually smaller but collectively immensely larger) benefits to a great many worse-off individuals. That seems clearly wrong. It would not, for example, be a good thing to take a dollar from each of a billion poor people in order to give a billion dollars to someone who was wealthy to begin with.

So, rather than discounting smaller benefits (or refusing to aggregate them), Parfit suggests that we do better to simply weight harms and benefits in a way that gives priority to the worse off. Two appealing implications of this view are that: (1) we generally should not allow huge harms to befall a single person, if that leaves them much worse off than the others with competing interests; (2) but we should allow (sufficient) small benefits to the worse off to (in sum) outweigh a single large benefit to someone better off. Since we need aggregation in order to secure verdict (2), and we can secure verdict (1) without having to reject aggregation, it looks like our intuitions are, overall, best served by accepting an aggregative moral theory.

Critics might respond that Parfit's prioritarian account cannot do full justice to our starting intuition about the Transmitter Room case. Granted, sufficient priority weighting may explain how Jones's suffering can outweigh the aggregate pleasure of a million, or even a billion, better-off football fans. But so long as the priority weighting is finite, there will be *some* amount of smaller pleasures (perhaps astronomically large in number) that could, in theory, outweigh Jones's suffering. At this point in the dialectic, I think the defender of Parfit's view should simply accept this implication, and suggest that any residual intuitive discomfort with this conclusion is best explained by our inability to truly grasp large numbers. Our intuitions do not respond very differently to whether the number of competing interests is a million, a billion, or a googolplex. But the real difference in value between these numbers is immense. So we should not trust our intuitions when they treat these vastly different numbers as morally alike.

In short: we may respect the intuition that one person's severe pain is not *easily* outweighed by smaller benefits for many others. But we've little reason to trust the more radical intuition that the one severe pain must outweigh literally *any* number of smaller benefits, no matter how astronomically large that number is.

You might be tempted to think that some benefits are so *trivial* that we should round them down to zero, rather than allowing vast numbers of them to sum to something morally significant. Parfit argues that this way of thinking is a mistake. To see why, consider the following plausible-seeming claim:

(1) we ought to give one person one more year of life rather than lengthening any number of other people's lives by only one minute. (Parfit 2003, 385)

One year is about half a million minutes. So Parfit invites us to imagine a community of just over a million people, and apply the choice described in (1) to each of them. Each person in the community would then gain one year of life. But consider the opportunity cost. If each time we had instead given one more minute of life to everyone else, the end result would be a gain of *two* years of life for each person. So the choice described in (1), when repeated in this way, results in everyone being worse off than they otherwise would have been.

This clearly shows that (1) is a bad principle *in iterative contexts* like that described above. Does it show that (1) is a bad principle even in a one-off application? That is less immediately clear, but we may be able to show this with further argument. Parfit himself appeals to a distinction between fundamental moral *principles* and mere *policies*, suggesting that only the latter should be contingent on context in this way. If he's right about that, this would suggest that our fundamental moral principles must allow for unrestricted aggregation, in contrast to claims like (1).

We might supplement Parfit's argument by observing that the expected value of each choice described above is *independent* of the other choices being made. The value of giving everyone one more minute (just once) is the same as the value of giving everyone one more minute (for the millionth time).[10] This is important for two reasons. First, independence implies that the expected value of the one-off choice is equal to the average value of the repeated choice. So, since repeatedly choosing *one minute for everyone* is more worthwhile than repeatedly choosing *one year for one person*, it follows (from independence) that the former choice is also more worthwhile in the one-off case. This is a surprising and important result.

The second reason why the independence claim is important here is that it can help to shed light on why this initially surprising result makes sense, and is (upon reflection) plausible. For, whatever valuable events an extra year of life would offer (all the moments of happiness, completed projects that would otherwise have been cut short, etc.), we should expect twice as many such events to be enabled by offering an extra minute of (representative) life to each of a million people. That is, after all, just what it is for the minutes in question to be representative of the people's lives, on the whole.

Parfit thus shows us that considerations of distributive justice, and of iterability, both count in favour of aggregative moral principles. Some critics (such as Voorhoeve 2014) nonetheless insist that giving some weight to the non-aggregative perspective is essential for respecting the 'separateness of persons'. Chappell (2015) argues that this is not so. The argument rests on two claims: first, the 'separateness of persons' is best understood as the claim that distinct individuals' interests are not *fungible*, or substitutable without regret, in the way that is true of "mere instruments" like money. Second, we can develop aggregative theories, such as utilitarianism, in a way that allows individuals' interests to be weighed, compared, combined, and traded off against each other, *without* thereby treating the interests as *fungible*. This is because, in choosing the greater interest, we may nonetheless have a distinct intrinsic desire (for the lesser

---

[10] There are ways of imagining the case where this would not be so. For example, if we imagine bestowing the extra minutes of life to each person on their deathbed, the first several such minutes might be disproportionately lacking in value, compared to a more representative minute of life. To properly test principles of aggregation, we should imagine a set-up where the independence assumption holds – for example, by supposing that the extra minutes are given to people at some earlier point in their life, before mortal illness strikes. This makes it clearer how a single minute might, in some cases, have significant value, by being just what the recipient needed in order to complete some important life project.

interest) that is thereby thwarted, occasioning regret. By separately desiring each person's welfare, utilitarians can thus respect the separateness of persons. When combined with Parfit's arguments, this result gives us strong reason to reject non-aggregative principles, despite their current popularity among many ethicists.

3.3 Individualism and Collective Harms

A different (but related) challenge to consequentialism arises from "collective harm" cases, in which individual acts (say of voting, or polluting) might seem to make no difference taken individually, but make a huge difference in aggregate. If each of us benefits slightly by polluting, and our individual contribution to the collective harm makes no real difference to the end result, Act Consequentialism would seem to have the implication that we each ought to pollute: doing so yields some benefit and no harm. Yet the global implications of everyone acting this way might be disastrous: *far* more harmful than beneficial overall. How should we make sense of such cases?

Parfit was extremely concerned about the systemic effects of our collective choices in the modern world, and gave a lot of thought to how misguided moral assumptions could lead us astray here. Parfit (1984, chapter 3) famously identified the following 'five mistakes in moral mathematics', which we will proceed to discuss in turn.

(1) the "Share-of-the-Total" View
(2) ignoring the effects of *sets* of acts
(3) Ignoring small chances
(4) ignoring *very small* effects on very large numbers of people
(5) ignoring *imperceptible* effects on very large numbers of people.

3.3.1 The "Share-of-the-Total" View

According to the Share-of-the-Total view, when a group collectively brings about some outcome, each member counts as producing their "share" of the total. For example, if 5 people work together to save 100 lives, each participant is credited with saving 20 lives. But if our moral decision-making were guided by this kind of accounting procedure, it could lead to foolish decisions with obviously detrimental results, such as:

(a) unnecessarily joining a group of benefactors (who together save 100 lives) who could do just as well without you, when you could instead have saved 10 additional lives independently, or

(b) single-handedly saving 50 lives instead of joining a group that needs you in order to save 100.

As these cases demonstrate, it does not really matter what "share of the total" gets attributed to you on the basis of the group that you join (as though group size were inherently morally significant). What matters is just performing the act, of those available to you, that results in the most lives being saved (or, more generally, the most good being done), in total. In case (a), you can bring it about that 110 lives are saved, rather than just 100, if you act independently. In case (b), you can bring it about that 100 lives are saved, rather than just 50, if you contribute to the group. These are the numbers that matter. No moral insight is gained by dividing any of these numbers by the contributing group size to yield some kind of agential "share". To think otherwise, Parfit argues, is simply a mistake.

3.3.2 Sets of Acts

Parfit argues that there are (at least) two types of cases in which it is crucial to consider *sets* of acts: overdetermination cases and co-ordination problems.

If two people shoot you simultaneously, it may be true of *each* that, had they not shot you, you still would have died (due to the other). Because your death is causally overdetermined in this way, neither shooter's act *by itself* harms you by making things go worse than they would otherwise have done. To understand the harm done, we must consider both acts *together*. Parfit argues that agents act wrongly when they are part of the *smallest group* that together causes harm, in the sense that if they had *all* acted differently the harm would not have occurred.

There are two important features to Parfit's principle here. First, it allows an act to be wrong even when the harmful effect was overdetermined. But second, it only counts an act as wrong if the agent would have performed it regardless of whether it was overdetermined.

To illustrate: suppose that Sam is determined to see me dead, and is sure to succeed within moments. And suppose that Jane is able to save another innocent life only by killing me first. So she does. It makes an important moral difference, on Parfit's view, whether or not Jane still would have killed me had Sam not been about to do so.

If Jane would have killed me regardless, then she and Sam *together* are the smallest group such that *both* would have had to have acted differently in order to prevent my death. Both would then act wrongly, by Parfit's principle. Alternatively, if Jane *only* performed this act because Sam was about to anyway, then had Sam acted differently (i.e., not been about to kill me) then I would have lived. Thus only Sam acts wrongly, by being the one to *counterfactually ensure* my death, even though Jane is the one that "killed" me in the ordinary causal sense. Strikingly, it turns out that "killing" in the ordinary causal sense is not what matters morally.

In overdetermination cases, it matters whether an agent's actions were sensitive to (or dependent upon) others' choices. This is also true of co-ordination problems, where the value resulting from one's choice depends upon how it aligns with the choice of another. For example, suppose you get separated from your friend at a crowded station platform, and then your train pulls up. Each of you wonders whether to board (and hope the other does likewise), or instead wait to find each other again before boarding the next train (while, again, hoping the other decides similarly). Perhaps it would be best of all were you both to board (supposing, for sake of argument, that you would easily find each other once on board), as then your plans would not be delayed. Second best is for you both to wait and catch the next train together. But the worst outcome occurs if you choose differently from each other.

Next suppose that the two of you constitute a surgical team, and the trains contain passengers who need your combined expertise in order to save their lives. If both of you board the first train, you can save ten lives. If both board the second, you save two lives. But on different trains, neither of you is able to save any lives.

Suppose that you both end up on the second train. Each of you is then in the position that, had you (alone) acted differently, things would have been worse. But this individualistic focus misses an important further fact: that by *both* choosing differently, the two of you together could have achieved a much better result.

Parfit thus concludes that it is important to consider sets of acts, not just individual actions (holding all others fixed). These issues were explored and developed in greater depth by Regan (1980), who concluded that an adequate moral theory must go beyond just requiring of us certain *acts* – it must also require certain *attitudes*, such as a willingness to coordinate with like-minded others, so that a group of individuals who successfully comply with the theory *together* achieve the best results collectively available to them.[11]

3.3.3 Ignoring Small Chances

A common moral error is to *ignore small chances*, and treat a sufficiently tiny chance of achieving some result as effectively *no* chance at all. For example, many people claim that it is irrational to vote, on the grounds that your vote "will make no difference". But, Parfit emphasizes, if a possible event would be

---

[11] Portmore (2019) offers a state-of-the-art development of this view.

sufficiently momentous, perhaps by affecting a sufficiently large number of people, even a tiny change in its probability could be highly morally significant. Consider nuclear safety: even if extra precautions reduce the risk of nuclear catastrophe by mere fractions of a percentage point, we usually recognize that they may nonetheless be a worthwhile investment.

The standard method of rational choice under conditions of uncertainty is to calculate the *expected value* of a prospect, by weighting the value of each possible outcome by its likelihood. For example, a 0.002 per cent chance of saving a million lives is, in expectation, equivalent to saving twenty lives. That's how many lives one would save (per gamble) on average over the long run, were the life-saving gamble to be repeated over and over again. This helps us to see that, if some option is not worth causing twenty deaths, nor is it worth causing a 0.002 per cent chance of a million deaths. To simply ignore this latter "small chance" would be morally akin to ignoring twenty (certain) deaths – a clear moral atrocity.

3.3.4 Ignoring Small or Imperceptible Effects

In Parfit's *Harmless Torturers* thought experiment, a thousand torturers each press a button that increases the pain of a thousand victims by an "imperceptible" amount each time it is pressed (Parfit 1984, 80). After a thousand presses, the victims are in severe pain. But has any individual torturer done any harm?

It is tempting to answer "no", on the grounds that what matters about pain is *how it feels*, and if a subject can't tell two experiences apart, they must (you might assume) really feel the same.

Parfit (1984, 79) rejects this implication, holding that 'someone's pain can become less painful, or less bad, by an amount too small to be noticed'. Just as the external world can change in some respect without our recognizing this (or *judging it to be so*), so we should expect that our "internal world" of subjective phenomenal experience might change in some way without our forming any corresponding judgement that this has happened. After all, when comparing our experiences across time, we must rely in part on memory mechanisms that cannot feasibly be expected to preserve every last detail of our past experiences.

So it is crucial not to conflate how things "seem" to you, in the sense of being *phenomenally present* in your subjective experience, with how things "seem" to you in the sense of being *believed* by you. It is not only logically coherent, but indeed entirely to be expected, that small changes in our felt phenomenology may occur without our judging or believing this to be so. Further, it is easy to prove that some such divergence must occur in the *Harmless Torturer* series. After all, in light of the clear phenomenal difference between the first and last pain states in the series, it cannot be that the thousand possible pain states are all phenomenally identical. So, by the transitivity of identity (that is, if A = B and B = C, then A = C), some adjacent pair of pain states must differ phenomenally – that is, differ in *feel* to the subject of experience – even if the victims cannot *tell* that this is so.[12]

We may further observe that the average increase in pain per increment must be one-thousandth of the total pain increase across all thousand increments. Multiplying across a thousand victims, we get that each press of the button can be expected to produce as much pain (in aggregate) as fully torturing a single individual. To ignore such an effect would, again, be a grave moral mistake.

3.3.5 Upshot

While Parfit uses fanciful examples to elucidate the underlying moral principles, his ultimate concern here is more practical. People routinely excuse inaction in the face of systemic problems (from climate change to democratic dysfunction) on the grounds that a single individual "can't make a difference". Parfit's arguments undermine this excuse. Even if an effect is very small, or we have only a tiny chance of bringing about some larger effect through our actions, so long as the affected population is sufficiently large (as is the case with many of the global problems that face us today), our acts may be very morally significant.[13]

4 Character and Consequence

Part One of *Reasons and Persons* (Parfit 1984) explores the different ways in which ethical theories may be self-defeating. Some goals, such as happiness, may be better achieved by aiming elsewhere. This "indirect" form of self-defeat raises important and intricate issues for thinking about consequentialism and action guidance. A different, more "direct" form of self-defeat may afflict ethical theories (including common-sense morality) that assign different goals to different agents: for example, directing each person to especially look after their own family members. On such an account, even if each person successfully does as they ought, this can (paradoxically) result in *everyone*'s moral goals being worse achieved. In this section, we will explore these two issues in turn.

---

[12] Kagan (2011, 132). (Arntzenius and McCarthy 1997, 135) make a similar observation about Quinn's (1990) "Self-Torturer" variant of Parfit's case.

[13] Such arguments are further developed in Kagan (2011), critiqued in Nefsky (2011), and defended against such critiques in (Chappell n.d.b).

4.1 Indirect Self-Defeat and Rational Irrationality

As Parfit (1984, 5) defines it, a theory T is '*indirectly individually self-defeating* when it is true that, if someone tries to achieve his T-given aims, these aims will be, on the whole, worse achieved'.

Put aside cases in which the agent fails due to personal incompetence or ignorance. The more interesting cases of indirect self-defeat are ones in which merely possessing the motive or disposition to pursue some aim tends to undermine the achievement of that very aim. How is this possible? Put briefly, behavioural dispositions can have causal effects other than just the actions they directly produce. They might change our available options, influence our emotions or other mental states, or change how others behave towards us.

Perhaps the most well-known example of this is the so-called *paradox of hedonism*, according to which happiness tends to be better achieved by aiming at something else (Railton 1984). For example, an egoist who cares nothing for others thereby lacks access to the happiness that genuine love and friendship may bring. Other 'essential byproducts' that resist deliberate and focussed pursuit in the moment include unaided sleep and spontaneity (Elster 1983, 43–52). In these cases, self-defeat results from how our own minds work. But Parfit is especially interested in "game-theoretic" cases in which self-defeat results from how others would respond to us, in a society where everyone's dispositions were transparent.

A transparent egoist, for example, could not be trusted to keep their end of a bargain and so would miss out on important gains from co-operation. If you hope to entice someone to help you by promising them some future reward, this will only work (given transparency) if you are truly disposed to follow through on the reward. But by that point in time, you've already been helped, so paying out the promised reward is no longer in your interest (supposing that the cheated party has no way to publicize or otherwise punish your perfidy). So, in being disposed to always choose the most favourable option of those available, you end up with a less favourable roster of options to choose from. In Parfit's (1984, 7) *hitchhiker* case, one may even be left to die in the desert for one's inability to credibly promise any reward to a potential rescuer.

These cases suggest that egoism can be indirectly individually self-defeating. Your self-interest may (in some situations) be better achieved by making yourself less purely self-interested. If Parfit's hitchhiker could take a pill that would make him always keep his promises, he would choose to do so since it would make him better off – even though it would also mean that he ceased being an egoist. This sounds paradoxical, but it isn't really. It's an open possibility that the most effective way to achieve some goal may be to change yourself so that you no longer seek to pursue it.

While most of us likely approve of promise keeping over egoism in any case, we should not rush to conclude that such "indirect self-defeat" suffices to demonstrate that an aim is objectively unjustified or irrational. (Better reasons to reject egoism were explored in section 2.) For on any sensible view of what matters, it's possible to imagine a situation in which the only way to protect what matters most is to make your future self insensitive to such reasons. After all, rationality leaves us vulnerable to coercion by those who would threaten what we most care about. Faced with such threats, Parfit (1984, chapter 1) argues, it would be rational to take a pill that rendered you (temporarily) utterly irrational, and hence impervious to such threats. So it can be rational (or aim-promoting) to make yourself irrational (or insensitive to the aims in question). Parfit calls this phenomenon 'rational irrationality'.

Similar considerations also apply in the moral realm. It could be virtuous to make yourself vicious. Just imagine that an evil demon will torture everyone forever unless you take a pill that will make you come to desire (non-instrumentally) that others suffer. Further suppose that the demon will similarly torture everyone if you ever lose your new malicious desire, prior to your natural death.[14] In that case, it's a very good thing (for the world) that you have this bad (malicious) desire. This brings out that we need to carefully distinguish two very different ways of normatively assessing desires. The malicious desire is *good* in that it serves to promote or *achieve* moral aims. But it is *bad* in the sense of *exemplifying* evil attitudes and dispositions, being morally misguided, or aiming at the very opposite of the correct moral aims.[15]

When the two conflict, which matters more? Should you prefer to achieve moral aims or exemplify them? Parfit thought the former, and I'm inclined to agree. Even so, it is worth recognizing *both* modes of normative assessment: it would be an impoverished moral theory that found itself unable to articulate *any* sense in which useful malicious desires are nonetheless criticizable.

An important upshot of Parfit's discussion is that a theory isn't disproven just because it's indirectly self-defeating. Here's a quick argument of my own to that

---

[14] Curiously, once you've acquired the malicious desire, it will lead you to try to rid yourself of it, so as to cause the threatened universal torture. This demonstrates how it could be vicious to make yourself virtuous. But to ensure that your initial moral corruption was not for nothing, let us stipulate that your evil future self will lack the means to lose the world-saving malicious desire.

[15] In Chappell (2012), I call this the distinction between what's 'fortunate' and what's 'fitting'. The malicious desire in our example is morally fortunate but unfitting.

same conclusion: any sane moral theory requires us to avoid disaster in high-stakes situations. An evil demon might require us to abandon such a theory, in order to avoid disaster. So any sane moral theory is *possibly* self-effacing in this way. But some sane moral theory must be the correct one, so a possibly self-effacing moral theory may still be the correct one. Further, the truth or falsity of a moral theory is non-contingent: it does not depend upon which possible world is actual. So even if a theory is actually self-effacing, this no more counts against its truth than if it were merely possibly self-effacing. So, a theory's being self-effacing doesn't mean it's wrong.

Conversely, just because it's good or rational to *acquire* some motivation or disposition, and even if it continues to be good or rational to *maintain* it, it does not follow that it is in any way good or rational to *act* upon the motivation or disposition in question.[16] For the benefits may stem from the mere possession of the disposition, rather than the downstream acts that it disposes you towards. The latter may be entirely bad, even if the former are sufficiently good to outweigh this. In our previous example, even though we should want you to acquire the world-saving malicious desire, we certainly shouldn't want you to act upon it, gratuitously harming others.

Parfit himself focussed on more prosaic moral examples with this structure, which he called 'blameless wrongdoing'. He asked us to imagine that a mother, Clare, has optimal motives, which include strong love for her child. This strong love sometimes causes Clare to act in suboptimal ways: providing a small benefit to her child rather than a much greater benefit to some stranger, for example. From the perspective of impartial consequentialism, Parfit suggests that Clare's act is still wrong, despite stemming from optimal motives. But he nonetheless suggests the following defence on her behalf: 'Because I am acting on a set of motives that it would be wrong for me to lose, these [wrong] acts are blameless' (Parfit 1984, 34).

This strikes me as a point on which Parfit may have failed to take sufficient account of his own lessons. Recall our earlier example of the world-saving malicious motives. If you act on those motives and gratuitously harm someone, just because you want to see them suffer, we may reject Parfit's suggestion that the optimality of possessing the motives renders their harmful exercise 'blameless'. We can agree that it's a good thing that you have the malicious motives, but that doesn't change the fact that they are *malicious*, or ill-willed, and hence in acting upon them you act viciously, which merits disapproval. Perhaps others should refrain from *expressing* their

---

[16] For further discussion, including exploration of whether we might identify a class of "well-calibrated" dispositions for which goodness and rationality *can* be successfully transmitted from *acquiring* a disposition to *acting* upon it, see Chappell (2019, section 5.4).

disapproval, as we wouldn't want you to lose your world-saving malicious motives.[17] If that's all that Parfit means by 'blameless', we can grant him this stipulative use of the term. But it's worth bearing in mind that this remains compatible with judging the present agent to be "blameworthy" in the ordinary sense of being *worthy* of moral criticism or disapproval. Just as the agent's motives may be doubly assessable, as simultaneously optimal and yet morally misguided, so too may our attitudes of approval or disapproval.

One might resist such judgments on the grounds that the agent's prior sacrifice was so immensely praiseworthy that any *overall* assessment of the agent must be positive. That latter claim seems right, but I am assuming here that we can offer a temporally "localized" criticism of the *present* agent, without thereby implying that they are eternally bad or bad *overall*.

The distinction between optimality and accuracy becomes even more stark when we consider that one can privately feel disapproval without in any way expressing this. For suppose that the evil demon will now start torturing people if anyone dares to – even privately – disapprove of malice. In that case, we had all best hope to have magic pills available that will allow us to cease disapproving of malice! But it wouldn't change the fact that malice *warrants* disapproval, in the same way that truth warrants belief, no matter how severely a demon might incentivize us to believe falsehoods instead. Consequentialists may rightly insist that some things matter more than having warranted attitudes. But they need not – and should not – deny these basic facts about warranted or accurate moral judgement.

Clare seems blameless in a way that the world-saving malicious agent does not. Since both agents are acting upon motives that it would be wrong for them to lose, *that* cannot be sufficient to explain Clare's blamelessness. So there is more work to be done in making sense of Parfit's cases.

I think we would do better to build upon the fact that, in loving her child, Clare's motives aim at something (her child's well-being) that is genuinely good. Even if she overweights this value relative to others, and so ends up acting incorrectly, she does not act with *ill will* when she prioritizes her own child over others. This may go some way towards explaining why she at least merits *less* disapproval than the world-saving malicious agent who gratuitously harms others. But if one further wishes to claim that Clare is *entirely* blameless, it may be that the only way to fully vindicate this intuition is to abandon impartiality, and hold that Clare truly makes no moral mistake in

---

[17] Perhaps it would even be unfair to your earlier, virtuous self to punish evil-you for acting in ways that were a predictable consequence of how you saved the world.

giving more weight to the well-being of those close to her. Such a move has its own costs, however, as we will now see.

4.2 Direct Self-Defeat

Parfit (1984, 55) defines a theory T as '*directly collectively self-defeating* when it is certain that, if we all successfully follow T, we will thereby cause the T-given aims *of each* to be worse achieved than they would have been if none of us had successfully followed T'.

As Parfit argues, theories that are *agent-relative*, giving different aims to different agents, are susceptible to direct collective self-defeat as a result of "Prisoner's Dilemmas". These are situations in which it's true of two agents that 'each could either (1) promote his own T-given aim or (2) more effectively promote the other's' (Parfit 1984, 55). Imagine yourself in such a situation. No matter what the other person chooses, your goals are better achieved by your "defecting", or choosing the first option. Symmetrical reasoning supports the other agent's choosing likewise. But as a result, both of you worse achieve your respective T-given aims than you could have, had you *both* instead "co-operated" by choosing the second option. (Your aims would be best achieved if you managed to trick the other agent into co-operating while sneakily defecting yourself.)

Parfit suggests that egoists need not be too troubled by this result, as their theory merely aspires to be an account of *individual* rationality, and it is not directly individually self-defeating. (Your choice of (1) is not detrimental to your goals; it is the *other* agent's choosing (1) that is the problem – for you, but again, not for him.)

Matters look different, by contrast, for agent-relative *moral* theories. For it is more plausibly part of a moral theory's job description to apply collectively, securing potential gains from co-operation in order to resolve such practical dilemmas. As Parfit (1984, 103) puts it: 'If there is any assumption on which it is clearest that a moral theory should *not* be self-defeating, it is the assumption that it is universally successfully followed.' But, remarkably, Parfit shows that common-sense morality falls short in just this way.

Consider Parfit's third *Parent's Dilemma*: 'We cannot communicate. But I could either (1) enable myself to give my child some benefit or (2) enable you to benefit yours somewhat more. You have the same alternatives with respect to me' (Parfit 1984, 97). Common-sense morality (M) tells us each to prioritize our own children, and hence to take the first option. If we both successfully follow this guidance, we will each have worse achieved our M-given aims than if we had both chosen the second option instead.

As a result, Parfit believes that common-sense morality requires revision. One option would be to accept impartial consequentialism. But a more moderate revision remains available. One could simply hold that *when* M is self-defeating, one should instead act so as to best achieve the M-given aims of *all* (so long as a sufficient number of others are likewise co-operative).[18] This principle has important practical implications for large-scale problems, such as climate change, where individuals may be tempted to "free ride" or prioritize their own family's material well-being, to the greater detriment of all.

In real-life cases, co-operation tends to coincide with benevolence, so it's easy to endorse. In hypothetical cases in which the two diverge, it's less clear that co-operation is such a good idea. Consider Yudkowsky's (2008) *True Prisoner's Dilemma*, in which you're in conflict with an alien paper clip maximizer about whether to save vast numbers of sentient lives or a few paper clips. The pay-off matrix is displayed in Table 1.

Table 1 The True Prisoner's Dilemma

	You: co-operate	**You: defect**
Alien: co-operate	+ 2 billion lives, + 2 paper clips	+ 3 billion lives, + 0 paper clips
Alien: defect	+ 0 lives, + 3 paper clips	+ 1 billion lives, + 1 paper clip

If you both co-operate, the result will be that more lives and more paper clips will be saved than if both of you defect. But when we consider your choice individually – whatever the paper clip maximizer happens to choose – your choice to "co-operate" rather than "defect" would gain a paltry two paper clips at the cost of a billion lives. Assuming that the other agent's decision truly is independent of yours, it would seem that the benevolent thing to do in this case is to defect.

One possible lesson we might draw from this case is that co-operation is of merely instrumental value. We often should co-operate, because that will often be how morally valuable goals are best achieved. But what really matters is the achievement of the worthwhile goals, not the co-operation as such. On this way of thinking, we might (contra Parfit) be willing to revise our understanding of the "job description" of morality to be less focussed on collective

---

[18] What number of co-operators is "sufficient"? Whatever is the minimum number such that, by co-operating together, each agent's M-given aims are better achieved than if each had instead just acted so as to achieve their own M-given aims.

implementation, and more focussed on the individually rational pursuit of *truly worthwhile* goals.[19] An excessively selfish person remains morally criticizable, on this view. But the explanation need not appeal to a flaw in their instrumental reasoning, or to their unco-operative disposition. The problem with the selfish person may simply be that they have excessively narrow goals or interests. They morally ought to care about others more broadly, and *want* better results for all.

5 The Triple Theory

Parfit's central project in *On What Matters* (2011a) is to argue that the best forms of Kantianism, Contractualism, and Rule Consequentialism converge, forming a unified view that he calls the "Triple Theory". These three theories have traditionally been seen as rivals. Rule Consequentialism directs us to consistently follow whatever rules would be impartially best on the whole (in contrast to the Act Consequentialist view that one should always perform whatever *act* would be best, even if that involves violating some generally beneficial rules in exceptional circumstances). Contractualists instead ask what principles everyone could reasonably agree upon, while typically eschewing justifications based on *aggregated* interests as morally illegitimate, allowing only "one-to-one" comparisons in judging who has the strongest moral claim. Kantian ethics, by contrast, revolves around Kant's exceptionless *Categorical Imperative* (in its various formulations). In this section, I will outline and assess Parfit's arguments for the convergence of these three great moral traditions.

5.1 Kantian Contractualism

The strain of Kantianism that Parfit develops is centrally concerned with *universalizability*. Parfit begins with a version of Kant's Formula of Universal Law, which he calls the *Impossibility Formula*: 'It is wrong to act on any maxim that could not be a universal law' (Parfit 2011a, 275). One important challenge for this sort of principle is that many acts that can only be exceptional (non-universal) are nonetheless morally innocuous: examples include giving more to charity than the average person, or buying only second-hand books (Parfit 2011a, 277, 284). Other acts, such as refraining from having children, or working in a non-agricultural sector, *could* (at least briefly) be universalized, but we might not much like the results. Even so, it would be a mistake to object to them on this basis, so long as a sufficient number of others are happy to do the necessary tasks: just because we need some farmers doesn't mean that everyone

---

[19] Although it may be a challenge to reconcile this approach with the lessons learned from co-ordination problems in section 3.2.

has to do it. These cases are importantly different from the disreputable sort of exception-making (such as free riding) that we want our moral principles to rule out. The challenge is to identify a principle that excludes just the latter.

Parfit eventually proposes a *Moral Belief Formula* (MB2) that holds acts to be wrong 'unless we could rationally will it to be true that everyone believes such acts to be permitted' (Parfit 2011a, 296). We can happily permit people to give exceptional amounts to charity, or to seek non-agricultural employment. By contrast, we have good reasons not to want everyone to feel at liberty to cheat on their taxes or pollute the environment (cf. section 3.3). So this principle seems helpful for isolating the morally problematic ways of making an exception for oneself.

One strikingly un-Kantian feature of MB2 is that it makes no appeal to the agent's *maxim* or motivating principle. The advantage of this, Parfit suggests, it that it allows us to avoid the 'mixed maxims objection' (Parfit 2011a, 293) that acting on certain maxims (for example, egoism) is only sometimes, but not always, bad. It also avoids Parfit's 'Rarity objection' to arbitrarily detailed maxims, by insisting that 'such acts' in this formula must be described 'in the morally relevant way' (Parfit 2011a, 297). Even if I *could* rationally will that everyone should feel free to kick people named "Bob" (this wouldn't, after all, endanger me or anyone I care about), that still wouldn't excuse my act of kicking Bob, because his name is not a morally relevant feature of the situation. Presumably, the deeper principle at stake is whether people should generally feel free to hurt *anyone* as they please, and – as someone who would not relish being on the receiving end of such violence – I certainly couldn't rationally will *that*.

I've suggested that MB2 may be a helpful principle, but it also raises further questions. For one thing, it presupposes an independent account of the "morally relevant" features of actions. We may often have an intuitive sense of these, but it is less clear whether this sense is sufficiently definite for Parfit's purposes. Consider the following: Will there always be exactly one "correct" description of an act, which precisely specifies what other acts count as being of the *same (moral) type*? If it is sometimes indeterminate what falls under the description of 'such acts' in MB2, then the principle may sometimes fail to yield a determinate verdict as to whether or not the original act was wrong.

Parfit's next major revision of Kantian ethics stems from what he calls the *High Stakes Objection* (Parfit 2011a, 332). Suppose that murdering someone is the only way to save your life. You might then rationally will that everyone should believe such egoistic acts permissible, since however bad that result would be for you, it's probably still better than dying immediately. Parfit's solution is to switch from asking what the *individual* could rationally will, to ask instead (in "Contractualist" fashion) what *everyone* could rationally will, or agree to. This then yields Parfit's *Kantian Contractualist Formula*: 'Everyone ought to follow the principles whose universal acceptance everyone could rationally will' (Parfit 2011a, 342).

But what if acceptance of a principle had consequences other than the downstream actions it produced? (cf. section 4). For example, suppose that if everyone believed that reading children's stories was immoral, then – magically – climate change would be averted. (Crucially, we are to imagine here that actually reading children's stories remains harmless. We merely have to *believe* that it's wrong, we don't have to act accordingly, in order to secure the benefits.) Why should the usefulness of those beliefs be at all relevant to whether their contents are *true*?

Perhaps Parfit could reformulate his Kantian Contractualist Formula to exclude these "side-effects" of our moral beliefs. But even then, as Rosen (2009, 86) points out, similarly annoying counterexamples could still be generated. Just suppose that gremlins would wreak havoc in the unlikely event of *universal compliance* with any moral principle. It would then seem awfully risky to will the universal acceptance of any such principle. But that wouldn't change the fact that some things are wrong. Perhaps Parfit could further refine his formula to consider what everyone could rationally will *in the nearest gremlin-free worlds* where everything else morally relevant remains unchanged. But such epicycles seem awfully inelegant for a putative "supreme principle of morality", and implausible as an account of what fundamentally matters. Rosen accordingly concludes that Parfit's Kantian Contractualism fails – or is, at best, something closer to a mere heuristic.

In fairness, Parfit does not claim that the Kantian Contractualist Formula describes the most practically important wrong-making property. Instead, he writes, 'There are other wrong-making properties or facts that would often have more importance. Our claim should instead be that this formula describes a *higher-level* wrong-making property or fact, under which all other such properties or facts can be subsumed' (Parfit 2011a, 369). If an appropriately revised version of the Kantian Contractualist Formula succeeded in unifying what would otherwise be a disparate array of wrong-making features, that would be an interesting and important result. But it remains far from clear whether it does in fact succeed in this ambitious task.

5.2 Kantian Consequentialism

According to Parfit's (2011a, 411) *Kantian Rule Consequentialism*, 'Everyone ought to follow the optimific principles, because these are the only principles that everyone could rationally will to be universal laws.' Let's put aside our concerns from the previous section, and assume, for the sake of argument, that Kantian Contractualism is correct: everyone ought to follow the universally willable principles. Is Parfit right to think that the optimific principles are uniquely universally willable in this way? We can break this down into two further questions: (i) Is it true that everyone could rationally will the optimific principles?; (ii) Are there any other principles that everyone could rationally will?

We can probe the first question by considering someone who would be disadvantaged by the (overall) optimific principles: perhaps their life, and the lives of their loved ones, would have to be sacrificed for the greater good. Could someone rationally will such tragedy upon themselves?

Parfit (2011a, 382) affirms a *wide, value-based objective view* of reasons, according to which 'we often have sufficient reasons' to act in *either* the way that is personally best, *or* the way that is impartially best. It is plausible that we aren't rationally required to be self-interested (as we saw in section 2.1), but are our reasons to care especially about family members and other loved ones merely *optional* in this way? Parfit (2011a, 385–89) offers a two-part answer: first, given that our chosen universal law is imagined to have (timeless) universal scope, it likely makes a *big* difference, and surely saving millions more lives throughout history could outweigh any reasonable level of partiality towards our loved ones. But this justification would not apply in hypothetical cases involving universes that exist only very briefly. And it is at least questionable whether such a deep moral question should turn upon such contingencies. That is, it seems odd that whether or not it's permissible for you to sacrifice your child to save five others should turn upon the existence of (unrelated) future generations. Second, anyone unpersuaded by Parfit's first move might instead resort to asking what would be chosen from behind a *veil of ignorance* (that is, if you didn't know your actual identity) in those cases where rational unanimity is otherwise impossible. But it's unclear what would justify forcing impartiality in such a way, if deep partiality is rationally justified.

While Parfit's arguments here are indecisive, many may nonetheless judge it plausible that it is always at least rationally *permissible* to prefer the impartially best outcome. The more permissive our conception of rationality, the easier it will be to accept this claim, but the more challenging it will prove to exclude competitor principles. After all, why couldn't some (non-optimific) deontological principle, such as one proscribing killing people as a means, *also* be universally rationally willable?

When Parfit calls a principle 'optimific' or 'best', he means these terms in the *impartial-reason-implying sense*, meaning *whatever* 'from an impartial point of view, everyone would have most reason to want' (2011a, 372). Importantly, this could diverge from typical consequentialist evaluations (of what maximizes impartial welfare): some deontologists claim, for example, that we all have impartial reasons to prefer that innocent people should *not* be killed as a means, no matter what else is at stake. This threatens to rob Parfit's "Kantian Rule Consequentialism" of much of its apparent interest and significance (Otsuka 2009). If it might be deemed "best" to abide by deontic constraints no matter the cost, the resulting view would seem "consequentialist" in name only.

Parfit might respond to such deontologists by invoking the *Deontic Beliefs Restriction* (2011a, 360–70): when applying a Contractualist formula to *determine* what is wrong, it would be viciously circular to appeal to *deontic beliefs* about what is antecedently wrong as one's basis for rejecting a principle. One must instead appeal only to *non-deontic* claims, such as claims about harms suffered or other features of the acts under consideration. Parfit argues that this restriction helps to push Contractualists in a more (welfarist) consequentialist direction. To see why, compare the following two competing principles regarding whether one may save someone's life by means of destroying another person's leg:

(A) *The Harmful Means Principle*: It is wrong to impose such a serious injury on someone as a means of benefiting other people.

and

(B) *The Greater Burden Principle*: We are permitted to impose a burden on someone if that is the only way in which someone else can be saved from some much greater burden. (Parfit 2011a, 361)

As Parfit notes, many people find the Harmful Means Principle to be highly intuitive. But if we apply a Contractualist formula to decide between the two principles, the Deontic Beliefs Restriction bars us from appealing to such moral intuitions. We must instead ask what *non-deontic* reasons agents could invoke for choosing between the principles. And now the defender of the Greater Burden Principle would appear to be on firmer ground, as they can appeal to the fact that loss of life is a much greater harm than loss of a limb (a claim that does not presuppose that any particular act is wrong antecedently to applying the Contractualist formula). This puts significant pressure on Contractualists to instead reject the Harmful Means Principle, and more generally to reject deontic constraints against utilitarian sacrifice – harming some in order to benefit others more. (Our current discussion focuses on 1:1 trade-offs between individuals; on aggregating the interests of many individuals, see section 3.2.)

This pressure may not be decisive, however. It remains open to the deontologist to insist that there are decisive non-deontic reasons to avoid acts that have a certain causal character, such as harming as a means. The plausibility of such a move turns on subtle issues. Parfit (2011a, 451) argues that when ethicists judge of some trolley case that it would be wrong to save five by killing one, they *first* judge the wrongness, rather than antecedently identifying non-deontic reasons against saving the most lives. He takes this to indicate that the reason not to save the most lives must stem *from* the wrongness as such – that is, it must be a *deontic* reason. Otsuka (2009, 54–57) responds that our moral intuitions (for example, about the wrongness of harming as a means) may instead serve to *guide* us to appreciate the significance of the underlying (non-deontic) wrong-making feature. It may thus be a non-deontic reason, *even if* we would not have recognized it as such in the absence of our moral beliefs. If Otsuka is right about this, it could undermine the significance that Parfit attributes to the Deontic Beliefs Restriction.

But even if his argument is not decisive, Parfit may still be substantively on strong ground. It would seem incredible to claim that the mere causal structure of a situation, *independently* of its making the act wrong, was more important than people's lives. It's awkward enough for ordinary deontologists to claim that the causal structure, *inasmuch as they believe that it makes the act wrong*, is more important than people's lives. But it is at least somewhat easier to make sense of assigning great significance to *wrongness* as such, or taking deontic reasons to be capable of outweighing the welfarist reasons to save more lives. It is, as Parfit (2011a, 398) stresses, much harder to believe that *other non-deontic reasons* could so outweigh immensely strong welfarist reasons.

This is, admittedly, more of a table-thump than an argument. But if understood as something like an invitation to share Parfit's moral sensibility having carefully reflected on these issues, it may prove reasonably persuasive nonetheless.

5.3 Evaluating the Triple Theory

When the best forms of Kantianism, Contractualism, and Rule Consequentialism are combined, Parfit claims, the result is his *Triple Theory* (Parfit 2011a, 413): 'An act is wrong just when such acts are disallowed by some principle that is optimific, uniquely universally willable, and not reasonably rejectable.' It is worth quoting at length why Parfit believes this result to be so important:

> Of our reasons for doubting that there are moral truths, one of the strongest is provided by some kinds of moral disagreement. . . . These disagreements are deepest when we are considering, not the wrongness of particular acts, but the nature of morality and moral reasoning, and what is implied by different views about these questions. If we and others hold conflicting views, and we

have no reason to believe that *we* are the people who are more likely to be right, that should at least make us doubt our view. It may also give us reasons to doubt that any of us could be right.

It has been widely believed that there are such deep disagreements between Kantians, Contractualists, and Consequentialists. That, I have argued, is not true. These people are climbing the same mountain on different sides. (Parfit 2011a, 418–19)

We can raise both "internal" and "external" objections to this justification for Parfit's project. Internally, Parfit's conclusions leave room for plenty of deep moral disagreement. Many influential accounts of morality, from Act Consequentialism to Virtue Ethics, are seemingly left scaling different mountains. Moreover, even if Parfit is right that the three accounts he focusses on coincide in this way, we might still dispute which is the most normatively significant. Are all three components equally essential? Or does one do the fundamental wrong-making work, while the others are merely incidental?[20]

Externally, there's plenty of room to dispute the claim that moral disagreement is as threatening as Parfit assumes. Chappell (2017a, section 3) argues that actual unanimity would gain us little of meta-ethical import. The deeper issue remains that there are any number of internally coherent alternative worldviews against which we can muster no non-question-begging argument. Whether those alternative views have *actual* defenders or not is irrelevant to how troubled we should be by them in principle.

So what it really all comes down to is whether it can be rationally defensible to maintain a view whose foundations might coherently be questioned. But this is something that anyone who is not a radical sceptic must simply make their peace with. Even the foundations of our most commonsensical empirical beliefs (that the external world exists, has existed for more than five minutes, and will continue to exist tomorrow) might, after all, coherently be questioned. If a radical sceptic disputes all our starting points, there will be no way to convince them that we are right. But we needn't be too troubled by such intransigence. What matters is not whether others might disagree with us (of course they might!), but whether they can offer positive reasons for thinking that some alternative view is more likely to be correct than our own. Sceptical doubts may prompt us to closely examine our beliefs, but they do not settle what we should conclude.

---

[20] Parfit does not explicitly address this question, though he does suggest that he considers Kantian Contractualism to be more fundamental than Rule Consequentialism: 'What is fundamental here is not a belief about what ultimately matters. It is the belief that we ought to follow principles whose being universally accepted, or followed, everyone could rationally will.' (Parfit 2011a, 417)

This stance is not (objectionably) dogmatic: we should always be open to the possibility of receiving good reasons to revise our views. Disagreement can be relevant when it's evidence that we've made a mistake *by our own lights* – a blunder we would disavow upon closer examination. But a *fundamental* moral disagreement instead reveals that you've met an agent who has different moral starting points from you. That might create practical difficulties, but it is not, by itself, evidence that your reasoning has in any way gone awry.

So I'm dubious of Parfit's convergence-seeking project. Methodologically, I'd sooner encourage moral theorists to develop the principles they find most plausible, no matter that others might disagree. Moving on to this question of substantive normative judgment, then, let's explore some reasons for rejecting Parfit's Triple Theory.

As we saw in section 5.1 (and back in section 4), it's far from clear that our moral evaluation of an act should indirectly depend upon our evaluation of some broader rule or principle. In particular, the mere fact that the best *uniform* (or universal) principles recommend an act does not mean that this *specific* act is any good – the principles' benefits may stem from other cases. This prompts a couple of deep challenges to Parfit's rule-based approach: (i) When an optimal act is ruled out by optimal principles, why prioritize the principles – why should acting optimally ever be considered "unjustifiable"?; (ii) Different people might do better to be guided by different principles – so, even on a rule- or principle-based approach, why require uniformity?

Parfit appreciated the force of the first objection, granting that the claim '(Q) all that ultimately matters is how well things go' is 'in itself very plausible', and would plausibly imply that 'it could not be wrong to do what we knew would make things go best' (Parfit 2011a, 417). This is why he thinks that Rule Consequentialism is better grounded in Kantian Contractualism instead. Surprisingly, he never explicitly rejects the foundationally consequentialist claim (Q), and as a result he does not actually conclude that his Triple Theory is the correct view. His arguments may be best read hypothetically: *if* you reject (Q), and are drawn to some form of Kantian or Contractualist view, *then* you should be led to the Triple Theory. It remains open to argue that one should then make the 'further move' to Act Consequentialism (Lazari-Radek and Singer 2020, 3) – or even, presumably, to skip Parfit's first step and just argue directly for (Q).

Against the second objection, Parfit (2016, 420) claims that 'everyone ought to have the same moral beliefs. Moral truths are not true only for certain people'. Here, it will be helpful to distinguish (i) the truth of a putative action-guiding principle from (ii) the higher-order normative claim that one should accept that action-guiding principle. These may come apart. As we saw in section 4, there's no guarantee that the true moral principles will turn out to be the ones that we ought (for practical reasons) to accept. So it could be true (for everyone) that each person should accept whatever principles would be optimal for *them*, specifically, to accept. The recommended principles need not themselves be true – a point that will become important in the following section.

5.4 Self-Effacing Act Consequentialism Revisited

In the third and final volume of *On What Matters*, Parfit (2016, 416) suggests that the *self-effacing* nature of Act Consequentialism 'might indirectly help to show that some other moral view is true'. This is deeply puzzling, contradicting everything we learned from Parfit back in section 4. He goes on to reiterate, more sensibly, that '[w]e should not assume that an optimific view must be true' (Parfit 2016, 418). But given this principled distinction between what is *true* and what it would be instrumentally *good to believe*, why should Act Consequentialism's self-effacing nature be of any epistemic significance whatsoever? Parfit never explains (Lazari-Radek and Singer 2020).

Perhaps Parfit was confused. Another possibility is that he was adverting to his subsequent argument that the wrongness of contributing to collective harms is 'best explained in a Rule Consequentialist way' (Parfit 2016, 433). Act Consequentialism would be disastrously suboptimal if it could not adequately explain our reasons against contributing to climate change and other massively distributed global harms. Such a failure would plausibly count against the view. But, even in that case, the true source of the failure would not lie in the suboptimality of *believing* Act Consequentialism, but in its (supposed) inability to adequately *account* for this class of genuine harms.

Why does Parfit suggest that Act Consequentialism cannot adequately explain the wrongness of contributing to collective harms? He writes that '[i]mperceptible amounts of pain, and other such harms, seem to most of us to be below any plausible threshold of moral significance' (Parfit 2016, 432). Yet we saw in section 3.3 that such appearances are demonstrably misleading, and that there *is* no such 'threshold' of moral significance: even the most minuscule of individual harms, when repeated over a great number of victims, can have immense moral significance. If the total costs outweigh the total benefits from all the contributions, then it must be that the average contribution has proportionately negative expected value, all things considered. So this seems to be another mysterious instance of the later Parfit ignoring the crucial insights to be gained from his earlier work (Parfit 1984).

5.5 Other Lessons

I've been very critical of *On What Matters* in this section, so it might be worth wrapping up by highlighting what I take to be some of the most valuable normative-ethical insights to be found within these weighty tomes.

(1) As explained in section 5.2, Parfit argues powerfully that the Deontic Beliefs Restriction should move Contractualists in a more consequentialist direction (rejecting deontic side-constraints against harming as a means).

(2) Parfit (2011a, chapter 9) offers a compelling objection to the Kantian assumption that utilitarian sacrifice (absent consent) essentially treats the sacrificed party 'merely as a means'. In Parfit's *Third Earthquake* scenario, we are invited to imagine that you save your child's life by using another person as a shield, crushing the other's toe without her consent. But we are to further suppose that you refrained from saving your own life, due to the fact that this would have crushed a second of the other person's toes. Since you value this other person more highly than your own life, you are clearly not treating her *merely* as a means, despite using her (without her consent) as a means to save your child's life. Parfit sensibly concludes that if your treatment of another person is sufficiently guided by relevant moral constraints (fully appreciating their value as a person), then you are not treating them merely as a means. This is an important corrective to this common objection to utilitarian sacrifice. It also threatens to trivialize versions of Kantianism that seek to ground all of ethics upon the prohibition against treating anyone merely as a means.

(3) Parfit (2016, chapter 56) argues against 'commonsense' moralists (and defenders of the Doctrine of Double Effect) who want to specifically prohibit harming *as a means*, while permitting comparably beneficial harms that are mere *side effects* (or 'collateral damage'). He shows that the very objections standardly offered against harming as a means apply just as powerfully against harming as a side effect. Either option equally harms the subject *without their consent* or, in the case of killing, robs them of *the only life they have.*

(4) Arguing against Thomson's (1976) principle that it's permissible to beneficially redirect existing threats (whether bombs or trolleys) but not to introduce new ones, Parfit (2016, chapter 56) offers a *Fire and Flood* scenario in which it would be clearly morally better to save more lives by flooding a burning building, killing one person in the basement, than to merely save a few lives by redirecting the fire into another room where five people would still be killed. Parfit concludes that we should all accept the following *Principle of Unintended Threats*: 'When there is some

unintended threat to people's lives, such as some fire, flood, approaching asteroid, or runaway train, we could justifiably do whatever would cause fewer people to be killed' (Parfit 2016, 392). This requires some revision of common verdicts in trolley cases (to permit pushing one in front of the trolley if that would save five). In other controversial cases, such as *Transplant* – killing one to provide vital organ transplants to five others – Parfit claims that his principle 'does not apply, because these cases do not involve unintended threats to people's lives' (Parfit 2016, 393). He unfortunately does not explain why organ failure, for example, does not count as an 'unintended threat'.[21] Perhaps he means to restrict the principle to *external* threats? Or perhaps to threats of which a single instance is capable of killing multiple people? More work may be required to pin down the best version of Parfit's principle.

All of this is, of course, just a small sample of the many thought-provoking arguments and thought experiments to be found in Parfit's work. Interested readers are encouraged to take a more thorough look for themselves. Even when you disagree with Parfit's conclusions (as I often have in this section), there is always a lot to be learned from engaging with his ideas.

6 Personal Identity

Parfit's philosophy is full of provocative, revisionary claims, and nowhere is this more true than in his treatment of personal identity. Parfit (1984, part 3) argues that we do not endure, or exist through time, in quite the way that we ordinarily suppose. He further argues that 'identity is not what matters', as one might split into multiple future 'selves' (in the relevant sense) without any of them truly being one and the same person as oneself. Such claims initially sound incredible. But, as we will see, they are supported by reasoning that is difficult to deny.

6.1 Reductionism about Identity

Suppose ten people start their own club. It eventually lapses, but years later one of them decides to reinvent the club with a new group of friends. Is there any fact of the matter as to whether this later club is *one and the same* as the old one? Parfit uses examples like these to support a kind of *conventionalism* – or what he calls 'reductionism' – about identity.

There is a strict sense in which everything is identical to itself, and numerically distinct from every other object (including those that they exactly resemble,

---

[21] Thanks to Jeff McMahan for raising this objection.

which we sometimes call "identical" in a different, qualitative sense: two qualitatively identical tennis balls are nonetheless numerically or strictly distinct objects – there are two of them, not just one). Common sense holds that objects can endure through change: a tree has fewer leaves by winter than it did in mid-summer, but it is still (one and) the same tree. Such thoughts can provoke philosophical reflection: *What does it take* to be the same object at different times? If the tree falls over in a storm, is it still the same tree? What if it is logged and turned into a raft?

These questions can provoke very different reactions in people. Some take them very seriously, as concerning deep truths about the structure of reality. Others take the questions to be superficial, merely verbal, concerning how we choose to talk about and categorize the world. Such conventionalism seems especially natural when talking about the identity conditions for non-conscious entities such as trees or clubs. It would seem incredible to claim that if two people had different ideas about the identity conditions for social clubs, one of them must thereby be making some deep mistake about the true structure of reality – as though such entities came with invisible name tags built-in, and we might be wrong about what name was invisibly written on such a tag. More plausibly, people who disagree just accept different conventions, and nothing in reality forces us to favour either convention over the other. But it is much harder to believe that the identity of *conscious beings*, such as ourselves, could be merely conventional in this way.

When I believe that some future person will be *me*, I *anticipate* having their experiences in future, and I have a special – prudential – kind of concern for their (my) well-being, seemingly different in kind from the other-regarding concern I might have for other people. Or consider a test-case, like *Teletransportation*: a machine scans my brain and body (down to the last atom), disintegrates it, sends the information via radio signal to another machine on Mars, which then reconstructs the exact configuration of my brain and body (all out of new atoms). The person stepping out of the teletransporter on Mars will have all my memories, beliefs, desires, and personality. They will self-identify as me. But is it really *me* who will step out on Mars, or have I been replaced with a perfect replica?

This seems like a genuine – and important – question. We may mock the idea of metaphysical name tags for groups and merely physical objects, but things seem different when it comes to conscious minds: *surely* there's a fact of the matter whether the person who steps out of the teletransporter is really *me* or just a replica. We can know all the descriptive, qualitative facts about what will happen in the scenario – what the emerging person will think and experience, and how the contents of those thoughts relate to those of the person who entered the teletransporter on Earth – but still wonder whether these thoughts, however similar in content, are being had by the same *thinker* as before. This way of thinking seems implicitly to presuppose the *Featureless Cartesian View* that an immaterial mind or soul *contains* our thoughts/experiences and grounds our identity. We can imagine losing all our memories and turning into an ordinary cat, for example, which is different from imagining that we are (destroyed and) *replaced with* a cat. The imagined difference presumably lies in whether the subsequent cat experiences are imagined to be contained within the *same conscious mind* that used to be ours, however different the contents of this mental container may now be.

What, though, would the identity conditions for such a featureless mental container be? It cannot be given by the contents, since, ex hypothesi, the container may persist through even the most radical changes in its contents (and, conversely, containers may be replaced while their contents remain unchanged, as in the case of a replica). But that leaves the identity of the container unmoored. As Parfit (1984, 228) objects (following Locke), such a view implies the possibility of brute identity swaps:

> [W]hile you are reading this page of text, you might suddenly cease to exist, and your body be taken over by some new person who is merely exactly like you. If this happened, no one would notice any difference. There would never be any evidence, public or private, showing whether or not this happens, and if so, how often. We therefore cannot even claim that it is unlikely to happen.

Could our identities all swap around, to no discernible effect, every minute or even every second? It's far from clear that such a scenario is coherently intelligible. And this may prompt us to reject the container view of personal identity. Even if immaterial souls existed, they would not be what grounds our identity.[22] What matters is the qualitative content, not the container. But then there is no deep distinction to be drawn between replication and ordinary survival after all. The question whether you survive teletransportation turns out to be no more substantial than our earlier question about the identity conditions for social clubs.

---

[22] Curiously, Parfit (1984, 227–28) denies this. He suggests that 'a non-reductionist view might have been true', had it turned out that there was reliable evidence of reincarnation. But this strikes me as a mistake. Even if we had reason to believe in immaterial souls that could preserve psychological content (such as memories and personalities) across human lives, there's no reason to attribute *name tags* to those souls, or to take personal identity to be a *deep further fact* grounded in such name tags rather than in content-continuity relations. It would be more consistent for reductionists to hold that, even supposing that Sally is Napoleon reincarnated, this fact (still) consists in nothing more than the relations of psychological continuity and counter-factual dependence that hold between the two of them. Ordinarily, our brains serve as the vehicles that underpin psychological continuity and counterfactual dependence between

This has striking implications in Parfit's *Branch-Line Case*, in which the scanner on Earth doesn't disintegrate you, but instead damages your heart so that you will die within a couple of hours (while your new Replica on Mars lives on). This is roughly equivalent, Parfit suggests, to taking sleeping pills that cause *retrograde amnesia*: 'if I take such a pill, I shall remain awake for an hour, but after my night's sleep I shall have no memories of the second half of this hour' (Parfit 1984, 287). Parfit explains: 'Suppose that I took such a pill nearly an hour ago. The person who wakes up in my bed tomorrow will not be psychologically continuous with me as I am now. He will be psychologically continuous with me as I was half an hour ago. I am now on a *psychological branch-line*, which will end soon when I fall asleep' (Parfit 1984, 287). This does not seem so bad. Even if your closest future continuant is only truly continuous with your recently past self, rather than with your current self, you could reasonably regard this as roughly as good as ordinary survival. So even in the Branch-Line Case where you are about to die while your Replica lives on, this too should probably be regarded as roughly as good as ordinary survival. It might be psychologically difficult to accept this. But even if we accept Parfit's reductionism on an intellectual level, our intuitions may fail to fall into line, much as we may feel fear in a glass-floored elevator despite knowing, intellectually, that we are perfectly safe.

My above container/content argument was loosely inspired by Parfitian themes. Parfit's own argument for reductionism invokes a different thought experiment, the *Combined Spectrum* (Parfit 1984, 236–37):

> At the near end of this spectrum is the normal case in which a future person would be fully continuous with me as I am now, both physically and psychologically. ... At the far end of this spectrum the resulting person would have no continuity with me as I am now, either physically or psychologically. In this case, the scientists would destroy my brain and body, and then create, out of new organic matter, a perfect Replica of ... Greta Garbo.

At intermediate points along the spectrum, varying proportions of the cells in Parfit's brain and body are replaced in ways that make the resulting person more and more like Greta Garbo. But the spectrum lacks drastic discontinuities. We can imagine a full spectrum of possible people, starting with pure Parfit, then Parfit with a hint of Garbo, through various mixes of the two, until we reach Garbo with a hint of Parfit, and finally pure Garbo. Parfit uses this thought experiment to argue that personal identity is *vague*, rather than being an all-or-

---

different "timeslices" or momentary stages of people; in the imagined scenario, immaterial souls can also play this vehicular role. But if we previously thought that personal identity was a matter of content-continuity relations (rather than vehicular name tags), it's entirely unclear why adding a second possible vehicle into the mix should suddenly make us rethink this.

nothing phenomenon. For early in the spectrum, it's clear that Parfit survives. By later in the spectrum, it's clear that Parfit is destroyed. But could there really be a sharp borderline between two adjacent points on the spectrum, where removing just one more cell makes all the difference to whether the resulting person is still Parfit? What could make it true that Parbo #721 was still Parfit, while the practically indistinguishable Parbo #722 was not? As Parfit asks, 'What would the difference consist in?' (Parfit 1984, 239).

The only plausible response to the Combined Spectrum, Parfit suggests, is to embrace reductionism. We can then respond to the spectrum cases as follows (Parfit 1984, 232–33):

> The resulting person would be me in the first few cases. In the last case [she] would not be me. In many of the intervening cases, neither answer would be true. I can always ask, 'Am I about to die? Will there be some person living who will be me?' But, in the cases in the middle of this Spectrum, there is no answer to this question. Though there is no answer to this question, I could know exactly what will happen. This question is, here, *empty*. In each of these cases I could know to what degree I would be psychologically [and physically] connected with the resulting person. And I could know which particular connections would or would not hold. If I knew these facts, I would know everything.

Many ordinary language terms are vague, admitting of borderline cases. They can still communicate useful information. But their boundaries are a matter of linguistic convention, and so cannot carry great normative weight. Often they serve to track some underlying scalar property that matters more (Chappell, n.d. b). (Imagine ordering a "heap" of sand, and then disputing whether the delivered quantity was sufficient. It would seem more productive to discuss the sand's mass or volume.) The Combined Spectrum seeks to establish this result for personal identity. It is not all-or-nothing, and so it makes no sense to have an all-or-nothing attitude of prudential concern. Our prudential concern should instead track the underlying relations of physical and/or psychological continuity, which come in degrees. On this view, the further along the Combined Spectrum you go, the less of a prudential interest you (the original subject) should have in the resulting person.

This makes an important difference to how concerned the subject should feel about the various outcomes along the Spectrum. Whereas the all-or-nothing view assigns 100 per cent significance to the border between identity and non-identity (and faces puzzles about where the borderline lies), Parfitian reductionists may assign only trivial significance to the difference between any two adjacent points on the Spectrum. On the other hand, they may regard larger differences as being highly significant even if they don't alter whether or not the resulting person qualifies as "you": going from 100 per cent to 90 per cent you, say, or from 10 per cent to 0 per cent. And this pattern of concern seems much more rational. Faced with such a spectrum, it makes sense to feel less and less attached to the resulting person, the less of the original "you" they contain.

We now have our first argument for why identity is not what matters: identity is all-or-nothing, whereas the Combined Spectrum shows that what matters in survival is instead something that comes in degrees – whatever relations of connectedness and continuity *underlie* our attributions of personal identity.[23] Parfit himself uses the Combined Spectrum thought experiment in a more limited way, just to argue for his reductionist view of identity. The further argumentative steps we're now considering are, however, a natural addition. Parfit agrees with the conclusion, that identity is not what matters. But he offers a different argument, to which we now turn.

6.2 Why Identity Is Not What Matters: Fission

Parfit (1984, chapter 12) famously uses thought experiments involving *fission* – or amoeba-like division – to argue that identity, as a necessarily one-to-one relation, is not what matters.

To begin, let's suppose that there is much more redundancy between the two hemispheres of the brain than scientists currently believe. For simplicity, we could even suppose that they are perfectly redundant: that you could survive the destruction of either hemisphere, to no ill effect. Next, assume that a "brain transplant" is better conceptualized as a full-body transplant: the person who wakes up is the brain donor (with a new body), not the body donor (with a new brain). Now suppose that the transplant process is a bit risky, so to increase your chances of survival in the face of multiple organ failure, doctors transplant each of your hemispheres into two separate bodies, Lefty and Righty. Consider three possible outcomes:

(A) only Lefty survives
(B) only Righty survives
(C) both Lefty and Righty survive.

In case (A), you clearly survive (as Lefty). In case (B), you clearly survive (as Righty). But what happens to you in case (C)? It is tempting to say that you

---

[23] In Parfit's terminology, 'continuity' involves *overlapping chains* of memories and other connec-
tions. The distinction is important for explaining the transitivity of identity: if A = B, and B = C,
then A = C, but C might directly remember being B, who in turn remembered being A, without
C remembering being A. Such cases suggest that the criteria for personal identity should be
formulated in terms of continuity rather than connectedness. But it leaves open which of the two
kinds of relation we should ultimately care about.

survive as *both* Lefty and Righty, but Lefty and Righty are two distinct people, so it would violate the transitivity of identity to claim that you are numerically identical to both. (If Lefty subsequently kills Righty, that is murder, not suicide.) On the other hand, it would be arbitrary to claim that you are identical to just one of them but not the other. So we seem forced to the conclusion that you do not survive: neither resulting person is you.[24]

In thinking about case (A), we find ourselves committed to the view that your relation to the surviving Lefty is sufficient for what matters in survival. Consideration of case (C) forces us to conclude that your intrinsic relation to Lefty is not sufficient for identity, as the latter also requires *uniqueness*, and thus turns on the *extrinsic* question of whether or not Righty *also* survived. We must then conclude that identity is not what matters in survival. That is, we can argue as follows:

(1) What matters in survival is something *intrinsic* to my current and future selves, and the relations (such as of physical and/or psychological continuity) between them.

(2) Identity over time is not intrinsic. Whether Lefty is me depends not just on him and me, but also on the *extrinsic* matter of whether another continuant (such as Righty) also exists.

(3) So, identity is not what really matters in survival.

Following Parfit, we may speak of "relation R" as the continuity relation that matters in survival. This is presumably psychological: as Parfit argues, since non-brain organs can all be transplanted without affecting our identity, we must ask what is so special about the brain. The obvious answer is: 'Because the brain is the carrier of psychological continuity, or Relation R' (Parfit 1984, 284). But this crucial effect might be achieved just as well by replacing parts (or all) of our brains with 'sufficiently similar duplicates'. Physical continuity per se does not seem to matter. Regardless, one who disagrees on this point could instead understand relation R as involving both psychological and physical continuity, for example.

If the R-relation holds (to a sufficient degree) *uniquely*, then we may say that the related objects are, in a certain sense, numerically identical: different

---

[24] An alternative answer that Parfit does not consider here is that your identity may end up being *indeterminate* between the two continuants. But this is not a deep indeterminacy, on the reductionist way of thinking; it is more like an accounting trick. We may *say* that it's indeterminate which of the two people you will end up as, but it's not as though there are two distinct possibilities between which reality remains unsettled – it is *merely* a way of talking. Reality is exhausted by the qualitative facts, including the continuity relations that hold between you and each of Lefty and Righty, which may all be perfectly determinate in the imagined scenario. Any further question of "identity" here marks a distinction without a difference, for there are no further facts for such a question to track.

temporal parts of the same temporally extended person. But on reflection, we cannot reasonably consider uniqueness to be all that normatively significant here. So, once we see that personal identity is just R-relatedness plus uniqueness, we would seem rationally compelled to replace our previous concern for personal identity with a better justified concern for R-relatedness. Fission is then no threat to your survival, in any sense that matters. You may not be identical to either of the resulting continuants, but you are related to *each* of them in every way that matters.

Lewis (1976) offers an alternative account on which identity remains intrinsic after all. It just turns out that there are *two* people (Lefty and Righty) who overlap, or share temporal parts, pre-fission. On this view, persons (and other physical objects) are four-dimensional "worms" that extend through both space and time. Much as conjoined twins may share some body parts, so may people who fission. After fission they are fully separate, but they overlapped in their pre-fission stages. Of course, when you stub your toe pre-fission, there is just the one pain. It isn't doubled, even though there are (or will be) two people who can count the experience as being part of their life.

It's unclear whether Lewis's view differs *substantively* from Parfit's, or if the difference is merely verbal. One crucial question, harking back to section 6.1, is whether there's any great significance in the boundary between being just *barely* sufficiently R-related to qualify as bundled together into the same temporally extended "person", versus falling just short of so qualifying. Lewis grants that the boundary is arbitrary, leaving personal identity parametric: one must simply stipulate what degree of relatedness one is taking to be criterial for bundling together into a unified "person". Such stipulations are, of course, entirely conventional. So I see no significant difference from Parfit's view here.[25]

6.3 Does Anything Matter in Survival?

Suppose we accept Parfit's reductionism, and the associated view that relation R (the right kind of psychological connectedness or continuity) is all that really matters in survival. Still, we may wonder *to what extent* relation R matters. Does it matter as much as we thought personal identity mattered, back when we took our identity to involve a *further fact*? After all, one way of characterizing Parfit's reductionism would be as a kind of illusionism or anti-realism about personal identity: you could say that we don't *really* persist through time at all – we can just *talk* as though we do, for convenience.

Here's a crucial question: Is it rational to *anticipate* experiences that will be felt by some "future self" to whom you are strongly R-related? Or does

---

[25] But cf. Parfit (1976).

anticipation implicitly presuppose a non-reductionist view of identity? Parfit (1984, 312) does not commit himself either way, suggesting that it 'seems defensible both to claim and to deny that Relation R gives us reason for special concern'. Of course, your "future selves" (or R-related continuants) are as closely related to you as can be, so if we have reason to be partial towards anyone, we presumably have reason to be partial towards them. But it would still seem a significant loss if we could no longer think of our future selves as *ourselves*: if they became mere *relatives*, however close.

I don't think such a bleak view is forced on us, however. The distinction between philosophical reduction and elimination is notoriously thorny, and analogous questions arise all over the philosophical map. Consciousness, normativity, and free will are three examples for which it is comparably contentious whether reduction amounts to elimination. Parfit himself took a firm stance on the latter two, viewing reduction as amounting to elimination in these areas. He notoriously insisted that we *need* non-natural normative properties, or else nothing would truly matter (Parfit 2011b). He also rejected strong compatibilist claims about free will, insisting instead that nobody could truly *deserve* to suffer, because they were not responsible for their own original character – however vicious it may be (Parfit 2011a, chapter 11). So it's interesting that he did not straightforwardly view reductionism about personal identity as amounting to elimination, instead suggesting that either answer here could make sense.

I find it tempting to give different answers in different cases. Consciousness and normativity strike me as sui generis phenomena, missing from any account that countenances only things constituted by atoms. For free will and personal identity, by contrast, I'm inclined to think that the "non-reductive" views don't even make sense (the idea of ultimate sourcehood, or originally choosing the very basis on which you will make all choices – including that first one! – is literally incoherent). Reductive accounts of these latter phenomena can fill their theoretical roles satisfactorily, in my view.

Other readers may carve up the cases differently. However you do it, my suggestion would be that reductionists can more easily resist eliminativist pressures if they think there is no coherent possibility there to be eliminated. If ultimate sourcehood makes no sense, it would seem unreasonable to treat it as a *requirement* for anything else, including moral desert.[26] So we might comfortably accept a compatibilist account as sufficing to make one responsible in the strongest sense, as there simply *is nothing more* that could be required.

---

[26] To avoid this amounting to a merely verbal dispute, I take it that reductionists and eliminativists must disagree about whether some putative reduction base suffices to fill an important theoretical role associated with the original concept.

Perhaps a similar thing could be said of personal identity. If we think that "further fact" views are not merely theoretically extravagant, but outright *impossible*, it might be easier to regard relation R as sufficient to justify anticipation. What more *could* be required, after all?

This reasoning is not decisive. Eliminativists could insist that anticipation is *essentially* irrational, presupposing something that could not possibly be. Or they could insist that the further fact view is not incoherent, but merely contingently false. Even so, their side too seems to lack decisive arguments. As is so often the case in philosophy, it is up to us to judge what strikes us as the most plausible position, all things considered.

The non-eliminative, reductionist view is, at least, much less drastically revisionary. (If our future selves are better regarded as entirely new people, there would seem no basis for distinguishing *killing* from *failing to bring into existence*. You would have to reconceive of guns as contraceptive agents. Nobody survives the present moment anyway, on this view, so the only effect of lethally shooting someone would be to prevent a new, qualitatively similar person from getting to exist in the next moment. Not so bad!) Though even if Parfit's reductionism can vindicate ordinary anticipation and self-concern, it certainly calls for some revisions to our normative thought.

6.4 Practical Implications

6.4.1 Long-Term Self-Interest and Morality

In section 2.1, we saw that Rational Egoism founders on the analogy between agent relativity and temporal relativity. That argument is further strengthened by Parfit's reductionism about personal identity, as your distant future selves are, in important respects, much like different people from you-now. If R-relatedness is what matters for self-concern, and it comes in degrees, it would make sense to feel less self-concern for your more distant future selves, as they are less closely R-related to your current self. Perhaps you should have increased moral or other-regarding concern for your distant future selves, the more that you regard them as almost like different people from yourself. But to suggest that you have reason to care about others besides yourself is to go beyond Rational Egoism, towards a more impartial normative view.

Interestingly, seemingly great imprudence (such as smoking) may then turn out to be more immoral, but less imprudent, than normally thought. Parfit (1984, 320) concludes, 'We ought not to do to our future selves what it would be wrong to do to other people.' If the future victim of lung cancer is effectively a different person from the present smoker, the latter's smoking can no longer be seen as purely self-regarding (affecting no one but themselves). So, seemingly "paternalistic" interventions to prevent such long-term harms might then turn out to be more easily justified, and not actually paternalistic after all.

6.4.2 Equality and the Separateness of Persons

A broader theme here is that Parfitian reductionism about identity undermines the distinction between self and other, or between intra-personal and inter-personal trade-offs.[27] Parfit suggests that distributive principles of justice might matter less, if the distinction between persons is less deep. On the other hand, insofar as uncompensated burdens are "unfair", reductionism might imply that there is more unfairness than we previously supposed, such as when burdening a young person for the sake of their much older "self" (Parfit 1984, 340–43).

6.4.3 Abortion and Dementia

Parfit suggests that reductionists can more easily account for fetal moral status gradually increasing by degrees, rather than being "all or nothing" – and can say the same, in reverse, of dementia cases (Parfit 1984, 322–23).

While I agree with Parfit that moral status can come in degrees, I believe he was mistaken about the relevance of his reductionism. Two importantly different questions need to be distinguished: (1) What is the nature of the presently existing entity – is it a *person*? and (2) What is the identity of the presently existing entity – is it still the *same* person as last year?

Parfit's reductionism only concerns the latter kind of question, whereas it would seem the former is more relevant to the ethics of killing. For example, in a dementia case, even if the original person has ceased to exist, if the current entity is still a person – albeit a different one – we presumably shouldn't kill *them* either! Conversely, even if a fetus is minimally sufficiently continuous with the future person to count, in retrospect, as "being" them, if it doesn't yet sufficiently possess the crucial capacities for personhood then it would seem to lack the moral status that could make abortion morally troubling. In either case, it's the status of the moral patient, not their identity, that seems to matter here.

7 Population Ethics

Parfit (1984, part 4) gave rise to the subfield of population ethics. Parfit introduced two problems – the Non-Identity Problem, and the Repugnant Conclusion – that have perplexed many philosophers ever since. In this section, we will discuss these two puzzles in turn.

---

[27] This is one way to address Rawls's (1999, 24) famous objection that 'Utilitarianism does not take seriously the distinction between persons.' For a different – distinction-preserving – approach, see Chappell (2015).

7.1 The Non-Identity Problem

An individual's existence is fragile – not in the sense that they are easily killed, but in the less-appreciated sense that they very easily might never have existed in the first place. We've all heard the cliche about a flap of a butterfly's wings causing a storm on the other side of the world. If such a storm changes people's behaviour in the slightest, it could easily change when subsequent moments of conception occur in the affected area. Different children would subsequently be born. Such reflections can bring us to see that we ourselves would almost certainly not have existed, had almost any major event in earlier history happened differently. (Should we then be glad, in a sense, that various historical atrocities occurred?[28] An awkward question to answer honestly.)

Our fragility is curious to ponder. But its greatest philosophical significance emerges when we turn our attention to the future. Our actions – and especially large-scale collective actions, such as a nation's choice of climate policy – do not just affect how well off future people will be. They also affect *who* those future people will be. And this creates a problem, because we typically assume that an outcome can be worse only if it makes some individual(s) worse off than they otherwise would have been. But identity-affecting actions make people exist who otherwise *would not have existed at all*. So they cannot be worse off than they otherwise would have been (since they otherwise would not have *been* at all). But surely there's something wrong with identity-affecting actions that result in greatly reduced quality of life for future generations? This is the *Non-Identity Problem*. To solve it, Parfit (1984, 378) suggests, we 'need to explain why we have a moral reason not to make these choices'.

Consider Parfit's (1984, 361–62) *Depletion* thought-experiment:

> As a community, we must choose whether to deplete or conserve certain kinds of resources. If we choose Depletion, the quality of life over the next two centuries would be slightly higher than it would have been if we had chosen Conservation. But it would later, for many centuries, be much lower than it would have been if we had chosen Conservation.

Suppose that, even in the case of Depletion, everyone who ends up existing has lives that are at least barely worth living. But the later lives are much, much worse than the different lives that would have been lived had we chosen Conservation. If we accept the *Narrow Person-Affecting Restriction* – that an outcome can be bad only if it is worse for those who end up existing (Parfit 1984, 394–95) – then we seem committed to the absurd conclusion that Depletion is the morally better choice than Conservation. It makes some people

---

[28] Smilansky (2005).

(at a minimum, those who already exist) better off, and nobody worse off. The particular people who end up existing, even centuries in the future with low (but still positive) well-being, would if anything have self-interested reasons to be *glad* that we choose Depletion, for otherwise *they* would not have got to exist at all.

Indeed, if you poll *everyone* who ever ends up existing after we made our choice of Depletion, they would *all* have reason to be glad that we chose Depletion. If we chose Conservation, by contrast, existing people would be worse off. Admittedly, distant future people might be more strongly glad of our choice, as they would get to live blessed lives. But depriving them of a blissful existence is no harm at all, so (on the Narrow view) this does not count against Depletion.

To avoid this absurdity, we must reject the Narrow view, and accept the surprising result that an outcome can be morally worse without being worse *for* anyone. In the case of Depletion, no individual is harmed, but the well-being of people in general is lower than it could have been, indicating that it is a worse outcome. There are two ways to vindicate this result. One is to appeal directly to *impersonal* value, such as the (total or average) well-being of humanity collectively. Alternatively, we may continue to appeal directly only to *individual* well-being, but (i) allow that existence can constitute a non-comparative benefit (if one's subsequent existence is positive on the whole), and (ii) allow that an outcome can be worse because some alternative would have benefitted people more – *including* those who, as it happens, now do not get to exist. This *Wide Person-Affecting View* (Parfit 1984, 396) yields similar verdicts to the impersonal view, but does a better job of capturing the moral intuition that it is individual people that ultimately matter.

Some philosophers worry that, if we grant that there is moral reason to want happy people to exist in future, we risk being committed to implausible procreative obligations. But this doesn't follow. As I argue elsewhere (Chappell 2017b), we aren't generally obliged to bring about good results, if doing so would be excessively burdensome or encroach upon important personal prerogatives (such as to bodily autonomy and reproductive freedom). The potential benefit to the future child is a factor to take into account when weighing procreative decisions, and it may help to tip the scales in close cases, but it is not by itself decisive.

A further possibility, to be explored further in the next section, is that the (non-instrumental) value of an additional life might depend upon what lives there already are. This is an implication of the *Average* view: if what matters is average well-being, then adding an additional life of average well-being makes no non-instrumental difference (and adding a life of below-average well-being would even be bad in itself). The *Total* view, by contrast, counts every additional happy life as contributing positively to the overall value of the world. Neither option, it turns out, seems entirely palatable.

7.2 The Repugnant Conclusion

On the *Total* view, the value of an outcome is given by the sum value of the well-being that it contains. So, when comparing different options, the best one is whichever results in greater total well-being. Given some natural background assumptions, this view straightforwardly implies:

> *The Repugnant Conclusion:* For any possible population of at least ten billion people, all with a very high quality of life, there must be some much larger imaginable population whose existence, if other things are equal, would be better, even though its members have lives that are barely worth living. (Parfit 1984, 388)

Zillions of people living mediocre lives sure doesn't *seem* better than ten billion in utopia. But it turns out to be remarkably difficult to avoid this conclusion (or something close to it).[29] Rejecting the Total view is not enough, for the Repugnant Conclusion also follows from the *Mere Addition Paradox* (Parfit 1984, chapter 19), to which we now turn.

7.2.1 Mere Addition

"Mere addition" is when we add additional lives – all above the baseline of lives worth living – to a world, without affecting the prior inhabitants in any way. Parfit claims, plausibly enough, that this process cannot make a world worse. After all, where's the harm? How could it be bad to add intrinsically good lives, to no ill effect for anyone else? This suggests the following principle:

Mere Addition: If the only difference between worlds A and A+ is that the latter contains additional lives above the baseline, then A+ is no worse than A.

Next, note that it can only improve a world to reduce inequality in a way that also increases total welfare, while holding all else equal. Call such a shift *"beneficial equality"*. Beneficial equality licenses the move from A+ to a world B where the worse-off group in A+ benefits more than the well-off group is harmed by the shift. If B is better than A+, which in turn is no worse than A, it follows – by transitivity – that B (a world of greater total but lesser average utility) is likewise at least as good as A.[30] We may iterate this process

---

[29] See also Arrhenius (2000).
[30] If values can be represented by the real numbers, then it further follows that B is outright *better* than A. But this may not follow if we allow for imprecisely comparable values, as discussed

until we reach the repugnant world Z, with astronomic total utility but minuscule average utility.

These implications may lead us to examine the Mere Addition principle more closely, and perhaps insist that A+ is indeed a worse world than A. Why might one think this? Well, for one thing, the addition of worse (though not bad) lives alters the shape of the world as a whole, and not for the better. Whereas before we had a world full of flourishing lives, we now find mediocre lives in addition. That's not to say that the mediocre lives are bad in themselves, or considered in isolation. But given how the rest of the world is, their addition may be considered undesirable.

Maybe. This response is far from costless, however. It requires us to reject Huemer's (2008, 903) *Modal Pareto Principle* (MPP):

> For any possible worlds x and y, if, from the standpoint of self-interest, x would rationally be preferred to y by every being who would exist in either x or y, then x is better than y with respect to utility.

Why? Consider *Benign Addition*, which is like Mere Addition except that the original population is slightly better off in A+ than they were in A. Then, since A+ would be rationally preferred over A by every individual who exists in either world, MPP implies that A+ is positively better than A. As before, it cannot be denied that the beneficially equalized B is better than A+, and hence that B is better than A. Repeat the whole process enough times, and we end up with the Repugnant Conclusion that Z is better than A.

MPP is an intuitively compelling principle, representing the idea that ethics is fundamentally person centred. There is a stark ideological divide between this *moral individualism* (which treats the value of individual lives as additive, entailing the Repugnant Conclusion) and the *holistic* view that rejects Benign Addition, against every individual's wishes, for the sake of such impersonal considerations as the world's "shape" or average utility. We will next consider additional challenges to value holism.

7.2.2 Value Holism

Despite its potential for avoiding the Repugnant Conclusion, Parfit judged the prospects for value holism to be dim. (We'll explore his preferred form of individualism in the next section). In this section, we first look at Parfit's decisive arguments against the simplest form of holism, the *Average* view, according to which the value of an outcome is given by the average well-being of the sentient

---

below. If A and A+ are only roughly comparable or are "on a par," then B may be an improvement over A+ while still being merely on a par with A.

beings it contains. We then consider further challenges that he raised against more complex, *asymmetric* holistic views, which treat the value of happy lives differently from the disvalue of miserable ones.

As Parfit notes, the Average view obscenely implies that it could be a good thing to add miserable lives of unrelenting suffering to the world, so long as those miserable lives were ever so slightly *less* miserable than the others that already exist. That would, after all, increase the average level of well-being (making it slightly less extremely negative). For a vivid illustration, consider Parfit's *Hell Three* (Parfit 1984, 422):

> Most of us have lives that are much worse than nothing. The exceptions are the sadistic tyrants who make us suffer. The rest of us would kill ourselves if we could, but this is made impossible. The tyrants claim truly that, if we have children, they will make these children suffer slightly less.

The Average view implies that we ought to have children in Hell Three. Clearly, this is wrong. We should consider it a constraint on any plausible population axiology that the addition of miserable lives must count as an inherently bad thing. The Total view clearly meets this constraint, but so might some holistic views that are more sophisticated than the simple Average view. One might, for example, hold that miserable lives always count negatively, but that the value of additional happy lives depends on what other lives there are (Hurka 1983) – leaving room for Benign Addition to count as bad overall.

Parfit (1984, 410) raises a further challenge to such asymmetric holistic views. A view that limits the value of extra good lives without limiting the disvalue of extra bad lives entails that a clearly worthwhile proportion of good-to-bad lives (for example, 10 billion to 1) in a population could constitute a *very negative* outcome – much worse than nothing existing at all – if the total population were sufficiently large. But this, too, is implausible. So we should allow sufficient good lives to compensate for bad ones, at least in many cases.[31] The tricky question is how to do this without implying either (i) that additional happy lives always add value, or (ii) that additional "compensated" miserable lives make things no worse. (It would clearly be better to have a zillion happy lives than to have those same zillion happy lives with one-in-ten billion *additional* miserable lives – even though the latter population remains positive on the whole, or better than nothing.)

So, letting "H" stand for a world with many happy lives added to our initial utopia A, and "H-" being like H but with proportionately few miserable lives

---

[31] In situations where Mere Addition is judged to make things worse, we presumably would not want such world-worsening additions – even of intrinsically good lives – to play such a compensatory role.

added, we want it to be possible to hold that *H is no better than A*, that *H- is no worse than A*, and yet also that *H is better than H-*. If values correspond to real numbers, this trifecta is inconsistent. But values need not be numbers. The values of A and H might be only imprecisely comparable, or "on a par" – like the creative genius of Mozart and Michelangelo (Chang 2016).[32] A and H- might then stand in that same parity relation, even though H- is straightforwardly worse than H.

Parfit's deepest objection to value holism is that it makes the contributory value of a life dependent upon 'irrelevant facts about other people's lives' (Parfit 1984, 422). There is some force to this objection, though holists will naturally reject it as question begging: their view is precisely that what other lives exist is *not* irrelevant to the contributory value of additional lives. This brings us back to the stark divide between moral individualism and value holism. Individualists might reasonably reject holism on these grounds. But in the absence of forceful *independent* objections to holism, it seems to me that one might also reasonably hold out hope for a holistic approach to population axiology that could vindicate our intuitive resistance to the Repugnant Conclusion.

7.3.3 Parfit's Solution

Parfit (2017, 154) defends the *Wide Dual Person-Affecting Principle*, according to which:

> One of two outcomes would be in one way better if this outcome would together benefit people more [in aggregate], and in another way better if this outcome would benefit each person more.

Parfit recommends giving more weight to the latter consideration, favouring the consolidation of well-being into a smaller number of lives (within reason). To block the value of aggregate well-being from giving rise to the Repugnant Conclusion, Parfit suggests we might further claim that 'great losses in the quality of people's lives could not be outweighed by any increase in the sum of benefits, if these benefits came in the [creation of] lives of people whose quality of life would be much lower. I have started to defend this belief elsewhere' (Parfit 2017, 157).

In a talk titled 'How can we avoid the Repugnant Conclusion?', Parfit advanced a principle of *different-number-based imprecision*:

---

[32] Gustafsson (2020) develops the related idea of 'indistinguished value' (an absolute counterpart to incomparability), allowing even the Total view to escape some forms of the Repugnant Conclusion.

When two possible worlds would contain different numbers of people, this fact makes these worlds less precisely comparable.

When adding lives of very slight value, Parfit suggests, the increased margin of imprecision might swamp the added value from their aggregate welfare, preventing the additions from qualifying as good *on the whole*. This doesn't vindicate the intuition that the repugnant world Z is positively *worse* than the starting utopia A, but it can at least accommodate the more moderate claim that Z is *not better* than A.[33] So the solution is limited in scope, but relies upon less controversial commitments than the radical holistic views we explored previously.

7.4 Conclusion

Of all Parfit's myriad philosophical contributions, his work in population ethics may prove the most enduring and influential. He drew our attention to incredibly deep and intriguing philosophical problems concerning future generations; he raised powerful objections against views that could otherwise have seemed compelling; and he suggested what he took to be a more promising line of response. Many may remain unsatisfied with Parfit's preferred solution, but this simply highlights the enduring nature of the problems he brought to our attention. As we've seen, there's reason to think that no response to the Repugnant Conclusion will be without significant intuitive costs.

8 Conclusion

Trying to condense Parfit's ethics into a single Element has been a delightful challenge. Much has been skimmed over, and there is (of course) much more in Parfit's oeuvre that I have had to leave out entirely. (Grab yourself a copy of *Reasons and Persons*, for starters, and you'll see what I mean!) But I hope to have at least offered a taste of what one can gain from reading Parfit: the insights, the arguments, and – above all – the philosophical *puzzles* that will stay with you, and may even lead you to see yourself – and the world around you – in a new light.

I'll close with an extended quotation from the end of *On What Matters* (Parfit 2016, 436–37), in which Parfit explains what he takes to matter most:[34]

---

[33] Again, see Gustafsson (2020) for the development of related ideas. It's worth flagging that these verdicts are incompatible with Huemer's Modal Pareto Principle, discussed above, though – unlike holism – they are compatible with a weakened version on which the universally preferred outcome must be *not worse* than the alternative.

[34] For further reading on Parfit's chosen themes, see Singer (2009) and Ord (2020).

One thing that greatly matters is the failure of we rich people to prevent, as we so easily could, much of the suffering and many of the early deaths of the poorest people in the world. The money that we spend on an evening's entertainment might instead save some poor person from death, blindness, or chronic and severe pain. If we believe that, in our treatment of these poorest people, we are not acting wrongly, we are like those who believed that they were justified in having slaves.

Some of us ask how much of our wealth we rich people ought to *give* to these poorest people. But that question wrongly assumes that our wealth is ours to give. This wealth is legally ours. But these poorest people have much stronger moral claims to some of this wealth. We ought to transfer to these people . . . at least ten per cent of what we inherit or earn.

What now matters most is how we respond to various risks to the survival of humanity. We are creating some of these risks, and we are discovering how we could respond to these and other risks. If we reduce these risks, and humanity survives the next few centuries, our descendants or successors could end these risks by spreading through this galaxy.

Life can be wonderful as well as terrible, and we shall increasingly have the power to make life good. . . . Some of our successors might live lives and create worlds that, though failing to justify past suffering, would have given us all, including those who suffered most, reasons to be glad that the Universe exists.

References

Arntzenius, Frank, and David McCarthy. 1997. 'Self Torture and Group Beneficence'. *Erkenntnis* 47 (1): 129–44.

Arrhenius, Gustaf. 2000. 'An Impossibility Theorem for Welfarist Axiologies'. *Economics and Philosophy* 16 (2): 247–66. https://doi.org/10.1017/S0266267100000249.

Chang, Ruth. 2016. 'Parity, Imprecise Comparability, and the Repugnant Conclusion'. *Theoria* 82 (2): 183–215. https://doi.org/10.1111/theo.12096.

Chappell, Richard Yetter. 2012. 'Fittingness: The Sole Normative Primitive'. *Philosophical Quarterly* 62 (249): 684–704.

2015. 'Value Receptacles'. *Noûs* 49 (2): 322–32.

2017a. 'Knowing What Matters'. In *Does Anything Really Matter? Essays on Parfit on Objectivity*, edited by Peter Singer. Oxford: Oxford University Press.

2017b. 'Rethinking the Asymmetry'. *Canadian Journal of Philosophy* 47 (2): 167–77. https://doi.org/10.1080/00455091.2016.1250203.

2019. 'Fittingness Objections to Consequentialism'. In *Consequentialism: New Directions, New Problems?*, edited by Christian Seidel, 90–112. New York: Oxford University Press.

n.d.a. 'The 2-D Argument against Metaethical Naturalism'.

n.d.b. 'There Is No Problem of Collective Harm: Difference-Making Without Vagueness'.

Elster, Jon. 1983. *Sour Grapes*. Cambridge: Cambridge University Press.

Greene, Joshua, and Jonathan Baron. 2001. 'Intuitions about Declining Marginal Utility'. *Journal of Behavioral Decision Making* 14: 243–55.

Gustafsson, Johan E. 2020. 'Population Axiology and the Possibility of a Fourth Category of Absolute Value'. *Economics and Philosophy* 36 (1): 81–110.

Howard, Nathan Robert, and N. G. Laskowski. 2019. 'The World Is Not Enough' [online version]. *Noûs*. https://doi.org/10.1111/nous.12293.

Huemer, Michael. 2008. 'In Defence of Repugnance'. *Mind* 117 (468): 899–933.

Hume, David. 1739. *A Treatise of Human Nature*. Project Gutenberg, e-book. www.gutenberg.org/files/4705/4705-h/4705-h.htm.

Hurka, Thomas. 1983. 'Value and Population Size'. *Ethics* 93 (3): 496–507.

Kagan, Shelly. 2011. 'Do I Make a Difference?'. *Philosophy and Public Affairs* 39 (2): 105–41.

Kirchin, Simon. 2010. 'A Tension in the Moral Error Theory'. In *A World Without Values: Essays on John Mackie's Moral Error Theory*, edited by Richard Joyce and Simon Kirchin, 167–82. Dordrecht: Springer.

Lazari-Radek, Katarzyna de, and Peter Singer. 2020. 'Parfit on Act Consequentialism'. *Utilitas* 32 (4): 416–26. https://doi.org/10.1017/s0953820820000126.

Lewis, David K. 1976. 'Survival and Identity'. In *The Identities of Persons*, edited by Amelie Oksenberg Rorty, 17–40. Berkeley, CA: University of California Press.

Mackie, John Leslie. 1977. *Ethics: Inventing Right and Wrong*. London: Penguin.

Mintz-Woo, Kian. 2018. 'On Parfit's Ontology'. *Canadian Journal of Philosophy* 48 (5): 707–25. https://doi.org/10.1080/00455091.2017.1381935.

Nefsky, Julia. 2011. 'Consequentialism and the Problem of Collective Harm: A Reply to Kagan'. *Philosophy and Public Affairs* 39 (4): 364–95.

Ord, Toby. 2020. *The Precipice: Existential Risk and the Future of Humanity*. London: Bloomsbury.

Otsuka, Michael. 2009. 'The Kantian Argument for Consequentialism'. *Ratio* 22 (1): 41–58. https://doi.org/10.1111/j.1467-9329.2008.00417.x.

Parfit, Derek. 1976. 'Lewis, Perry, and What Matters'. In *The Identities of Persons*, edited by Amelie Rorty, 91–108. Berkeley, CA: University of California Press.

1984. *Reasons and Persons*. Reprint. New York: Oxford University Press, 1987.

1997. 'Equality and Priority'. *Ratio* 10 (3): 202–21.

2003. 'Justifiability to Each Person'. *Ratio* 16 (4): 368–90.

2011a. *On What Matters: Volume One*. Oxford: Oxford University Press.

2011b. *On What Matters: Volume Two*. Oxford: Oxford University Press.

2016. *On What Matters: Volume Three*. Oxford: Oxford University Press.

2017. 'Future People, the Non-Identity Problem, and Person-Affecting Principles'. *Philosophy and Public Affairs* 45 (2): 118–57. https://doi.org/10.1111/papa.12088.

Portmore, Douglas W. 2019. 'Consequentialism and Coordination: How Traditional Consequentialism Has an Attitude Problem'. In *Consequentialism: New Directions, New Problems*, edited by Christian Seidel, 71–89. New York: Oxford University Press.

Quinn, Warren S. 1990. 'The Puzzle of the Self-Torturer'. *Philosophical Studies* 59 (1): 79–90.

Railton, Peter. 1984. 'Alienation, Consequentialism, and the Demands of Morality'. *Philosophy and Public Affairs* 13 (2): 134–71.

Rawls, John. 1999. *A Theory of Justice*. Revised edition. Cambridge, MA: Belknap Press of Harvard University Press.

Regan, Donald H. 1980. *Utilitarianism and Co-Operation*. Oxford: Oxford University Press.

Roojen, Mark van. 2017. 'Derek Parfit: On What Matters, Volume III'. *Notre Dame Philosophical Reviews*. https://ndpr.nd.edu/news/on-what-matters-volume-iii/.

Rosen, Gideon. 2009. 'Might Kantian Contractualism Be the Supreme Principle of Morality?'. *Ratio* 22 (1): 78–97. https://doi.org/10.1111/j.1467-9329.2008.00419.x.

Scanlon, Thomas M. 1998. *What We Owe to Each Other*. Cambridge, MA: Belknap Press of Harvard University Press.

Scanlon, T. M. 2014. *Being Realistic About Reasons*. New York: Oxford University Press.

Sidgwick, Henry. 1907. *The Methods of Ethics*. Seventh edition. London: Macmillan.

Singer, Peter. 2009. *The Life You Can Save: Acting Now to Stop World Poverty*. New York: Random House.

Skorupski, John. 2010. *The Domain of Reasons*. New York: Oxford University Press.

Smilansky, Saul. 2005. 'On Not Being Sorry about the Morally Bad'. *Philosophy* 80 (2): 261–65. https://doi.org/10.1017/S0031819105000264.

Smith, Michael. 1994. *The Moral Problem*. Oxford: Blackwell.

Sobel, David. 2011. 'Parfit's Case against Subjectivism'. In *Oxford Studies in Metaethics, Volume 6*, edited by Russ Shafer-Landau. Oxford: Oxford University Press.

Suikkanen, Jussi. 2017. 'Non-Realist Cognitivism, Truth and Objectivity'. *Acta Analytica* 32 (2): 193–212. https://doi.org/10.1007/s12136-016-0300-5.

Thomson, Judith Jarvis. 1976. 'Killing, Letting Die, and the Trolley Problem'. *The Monist* 59 (2): 204–17. https://doi.org/10.5840/monist197659224.

Voorhoeve, Alex. 2014. 'How Should We Aggregate Competing Claims?'. *Ethics* 125 (1): 64–87.

Williams, Bernard. 1981. 'Internal and External Reasons'. In *Moral Luck: Philosophical Papers, 1973–1980*. Cambridge, UK: Cambridge University Press.

Yudkowsky, Eliezer. 2008. 'The True Prisoner's Dilemma'. http://lesswrong.com/lw/tn/the_true_prisoners_dilemma/.

Acknowledgements

My deepest thanks to Ben Eggleston, Simon Kirchin, Jeff McMahan, Peter Singer, and Helen Yetter-Chappell, for detailed and immensely valuable feedback. I'm also grateful for helpful comments and suggestions from Tomi Francis, Johan Gustafsson, Nick Laskowski, Dale Miller, Kian Mintz-Woo, Douglas Portmore, Carl Shulman, and Pablo Stafforini. Finally, I thank the University of Miami Fellowship in the Arts and Humanities for supporting my work on this project.

Cambridge Elements ☰

Ethics

Ben Eggleston
University of Kansas

Ben Eggleston is a professor of philosophy at the University of Kansas. He is the editor of John Stuart Mill, *Utilitarianism: With Related Remarks from Mill's Other Writings* (Hackett, 2017) and a co-editor of *Moral Theory and Climate Change: Ethical Perspectives on a Warming Planet* (Routledge, 2020), *The Cambridge Companion to Utilitarianism* (Cambridge, 2014), and *John Stuart Mill and the Art of Life* (Oxford, 2011). He is also the author of numerous articles and book chapters on various topics in ethics.

Dale E. Miller
Old Dominion University, Virginia

Dale E. Miller is a professor of philosophy at Old Dominion University. He is the author of *John Stuart Mill: Moral, Social and Political Thought* (Polity, 2010) and a co-editor of *Moral Theory and Climate Change: Ethical Perspectives on a Warming Planet* (Routledge, 2020), *A Companion to Mill* (Blackwell, 2017), *The Cambridge Companion to Utilitarianism* (Cambridge, 2014), *John Stuart Mill and the Art of Life* (Oxford, 2011), and *Morality, Rules, and Consequences: A Critical Reader* (Edinburgh, 2000). He is also the editor-in-chief of *Utilitas*, and the author of numerous articles and book chapters on various topics in ethics broadly construed.

About the Series

This Elements series provides an extensive overview of major figures, theories, and concepts in the field of ethics. Each entry in the series acquaints students with the main aspects of its topic while articulating the author's distinctive viewpoint in a manner that will interest researchers.

Cambridge Elements ≡

Ethics

.

Printed in the United States
by Baker & Taylor Publisher Services